THE CREATIVE WOMAN'S

GETTING–IT–ALL–TOGETHER *at home* HANDBOOK

by Jean Ray Laury

VNR VAN NOSTRAND REINHOLD COMPANY
New York Cincinnati Toronto London Melbourne

Acknowledgments

My warmest thanks go to my friends and students who inspired this book, and to all the artists who so generously and willingly shared their thoughts (and fears), their experiences, and their time.

I thank Nancy Newman Green for her skillful and thoughtful editing and for remaining both enthusiastic and patient through the long process.

Finally, I specially appreciate the valuable insights offered by Frank Laury in the early stages of this writing.

The quotation on page 12
Copyright © 1975 by Erica Mann Jong
Reprinted by permission of the Sterling Lord Agency, Inc.

Copyright © 1977 by Litton Educational Publishing, Inc.
Library of Congress Catalog Card Number 77-20224
ISBN 0-442-24704-4 (paper)

Published in 1977 by Van Nostrand Reinhold Company
A division of Litton Educational Publishing, Inc.
450 West 33rd Street, New York, NY 10001, U.S.A.

Van Nostrand Reinhold Limited
1410 Birchmount Road, Scarborough, Ontario M1P 2E7, Canada

Van Nostrand Reinhold Australia Pty. Limited
17 Queen Street, Mitcham, Victoria 3132, Australia

Van Nostrand Reinhold Company Limited
Molly Millars Lane, Wokingham, Berkshire, England

16 15 14 13 12 11 10 9 8 7 6 5 4 3 2 1

Library of Congress Cataloging in Publication Data

Laury, Jean Ray.
   The creative woman's getting-it-all-together at home handbook.

   Includes index.
   1. Home economics.   2. Artisans.   3. Housewives.
4. Time allocation.   I. Title.
TX147.L38   640   77-20224
ISBN 0-442-24704-4

Contents

Introduction   4

1. *Finding Time*   9
2. *Finding Space*   22
3. *On Being Superwoman*   31
4. *The Playpen in the Studio*   44
5. *Coping With the Mess*   58
6. *Shifting Gears*   71
7. *Getting Started*   82
8. *Coping With Deadlines*   94
9. *Supporting Yourself*   104
Note   137
Index   143

"I try to accomplish something artistic every day even if I have only a few minutes."

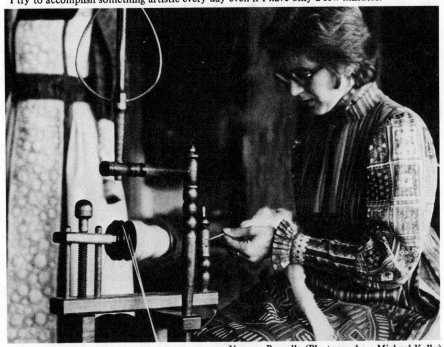

Yvonne Porcella (Photographer: Michael Kelly)

Introduction

There is a lot of sifting and stirring going on in kitchens today and not all of it goes into the muffins. Priority-shifting has prompted many women to shut the door to the laundry or pantry and open the door to a studio. A diminishing concern about the brightness of their washes allows more time for their creative work. One result of this stirring and sifting is a blending of roles, a mixing of ingredients which may not always be compatible.

The combination of roles in which a woman performs as artist/mother/home-maker/wife requires a tremendous amount of "getting it all together." How does she manage? She finds no set formulas. While no one woman knows *everything* about getting it together, every woman knows *something* about it. Obviously, by pooling our "somethings" we have access to a lot of information and an opportunity to discover some new perspectives on ourselves.

Abundantly creative women all over the country are producing work under varying conditions and pressures. Some artists flower working full time in studios away from home, but most of them create their work at the kitchen table with children scampering underfoot, dinner simmering on the stove, and a husband observing (somewhat apprehensively) the creative milieu.

What motivates the creative woman? Where does she learn to juggle her various roles? Can she successfully combine a serious, professional career with homemaking and child-rearing?

Here are responses from women of all ages, at various stages in their careers, who have achieved differing degrees of success. Most are involved with fiber arts as well as with teaching, designing, photographing, writing, or lecturing. Yet their comments seem equally applicable to women in all areas of creative work which are pursued individually. The painter, musician, poet, composer, illustrator, or sculptor will find much that pertains to her. The woman who manages any small business, publication, mail-order or free-lance work will also find parallels. Portions of the book deal with the pressures on any working woman, whether she works in her home or away.

Many fiber artists have contributed to this book in writing, through conversations, and in group discussions. Their willingness to share their experiences in an open, perceptive, and honest way has been overwhelming and touching. It is their purpose and mine to help other women find pleasure in meeting to some greater degree their own creative needs, to help them recognize their alternatives, and (perhaps most of all) to let them know that their problems and frustrations are not isolated and individual, but are shared by all women who combine creative pursuits with some of the more traditional woman's roles.

The woman involved in fibers as a career has a full-time job. If she also manages a home and has a husband or partner she has at least two full-time jobs. If there are children, in addition, her multifaceted activities are expanded many times over. While any one role may offer great joy and personal satisfaction, the combination of several roles may be a source of conflict. Most of us thoroughly enjoy these assorted passions and pursuits—but not without occasional clashes or head-on collisions. Not all the issues can always be peacefully resolved.

In the past few years, traveling from Seattle to San Diego, from New Orleans to Boston, I have been lecturing and giving workshops in fiber arts. It has offered me an opportunity to meet women coast to coast, from students to grandmothers, in community colleges and universities, crafts groups, stitchery and embroidery guilds, women's clubs, needlework shops and adult education, in rural communities and metropolitan areas. Talking to them has given me an awareness of some of the problems they face when they realize that being chief of diapers or the executive manager of the dishwashing and vacuuming equipment does not necessarily culminate in "living happily ever after." They are primarily inventive, energetic, talented women devoted to their families and seeking outlets for their creative drives. There are always a few who are thwarted, tired, or frustrated in those efforts. Some are ardent feminists, refusing to accept standard and stereotyped feminine roles. Others are wives and mothers working within the most conventional structures. But the questions they ask and the problems they face are remarkably similar. They share parallel needs, doubts, and concerns.

One common concern expressed by these women is a need to be involved in creative work when one is already committed to home and family. Very often the strength of the need is not realized until the opportunity or time for it is curtailed or practically nonexistent. It matters little if your living is shared with a partner, roommate, or husband—there are similar responsibilities in any long-term relationship. Children, no matter whose they are, require huge amounts of time and energy from somebody. These commitments make it more difficult to bring additional dimensions into an already packed routine.

Some artists know before they venture gingerly into junior high or pitch headlong into adolescence what they are going to do with their lives. Having made the decision early they encounter fewer conflicts; they consider marriage and family in the light of career interests, and occasionally exclude them outright. If you know yourself that well before you emerge from the gangly stage, you are unusual, fortunate, and probably aren't reading this book. But many women, at 32, with three small children and numerous volunteer commitments, hear the alarm one morning and realize they are not eager about the day. All is not well. That art major in college ten years earlier really *was* important.

Older women, having put off any serious pursuit of their own work until a time when they would be free of overwhelming family responsibilities, find that the "free" time never materializes. Awareness dawns that some retired husbands are as dependent as children. The need to be creatively productive remains. The myth that woman's total fulfillment comes in devoting herself to home and family explodes. The really successful mother is, after all, dispensable. She will have taught her children to become self-sufficient and independent. If her fabric-cutting scissors are already in hand, she'll find it much easier to snip the apron strings.

Retrenching or shifting gears is more difficult than establishing priorities early. Any woman with little working experience in the arts may fail to realize what potential she has for creating. But once she recognizes or even suspects this potential, it needs to be explored and fulfilled. It does not fade silently away into the night.

While there are no ready answers or easy solutions, this book offers a variety of ideas designed to help. Some women whose thoughts are contained here pondered their problems for years before resolving them; others stumbled over or blundered into workable solutions. Included are the lessons of my own errors and misjudgments (which may help you to avoid stepping into some of those same sticky places) and of my successes (which may help you to find an enjoyable balance). I've managed to evolve, as countless women have, a way to combine a full-time career at home with full-time family commitments. It has been hard work, but it has been worth it.

The problems of working mothers have long been recognized and scrutinized. But fiber artists who are also mothers encounter a somewhat different set of challenges. Income is not usually the crucial factor and their work is seldom pursued solely as a matter of economic survival. Given society's attitude toward art in general, and fiber or needle arts specifically, most women can see right off that the likelihood of self-support in fibers is largely fantasy. In related fields, yes—but to succeed financially in the fiber field alone requires a tremendous output in time and energy, as well as a talent which is both unusual and marketable. It *can* be done: there are full-time, self-supporting fiber artists. Most, however, are only partially self-supporting, or they also teach, write, or work in related fields.

The woman who is managing a home and bringing up children is usually involved in an economic arrangement with her partner: she is doing her part in a family entity, which entitles her to share in the rewards as well as the responsibilities of the "breadwinner." The role of housewife, however, may not give her the sense of self-worth that accompanies careers recognized by society as valid and worthwhile. Homemaking does not necessarily satisfy her personal needs for creative outlets. Even the woman who chooses to be a wife and mother exclusively can often be heard saying, "I'm just a housewife," or "I'm not working," or "I don't do anything."

Pursuing a fiber career while managing family and home is possible—many women have found they can have their cake and eat it too. They have to bake it, of course, and do the cleaning up afterward.

The nature of fiber work is such that it *can* be pursued at home. It is an individual effort, not requiring an office, affiliation with a company, or even a studio. Freelance work and exhibitions leave one without direct attachment, and the commitments vary. It is *possible* to combine fiber arts with homemaking and child-rearing. Nobody says it is simple, but it's possible. Nobody says it isn't worth all the effort, either, to approach fibers in a serious, professional way at home. It allows women who enjoy their children to be with them. It avoids many of the conflicts and guilts imposed by oneself, by one's family, relatives, friends, and society on women whose jobs outside the home remove them from the 24-hour around-the-clock demands of small children.

Another aspect of a home-studio is the degree of isolation which some women experience. Fiber artists often have little exchange with other women, particularly other artists. It is reinforcing to know that problems of isolation are not unique, and it's a help to hear other's solutions. This book proposes to help bridge a communications gap among women working alone.

Sometimes it is not possible to combine homemaking with a career in art. Some husbands *do* object: obviously, the women who have deliberately put aside their art work to meet the wishes or demands of family or husbands have not been contacted regarding this book, since they are not known through their art. There is no way to identify them.

Finally, working at home has the advantage of avoiding the burdens of transportation, lunches, nurseries or child care, and wardrobe. The homemaker is freed of the necessity to produce art that will sell. This is especially important for those artists involved in exploratory, innovative, and not necessarily saleable work. It allows time for personal development and growth which many artists find critical to their own artistic development.

Each of us searches for some measure of happiness, or at least some moments of joy in life. These are not remote goals. Happiness, joy, and pleasure are simply the by-products of day-to-day living. They rise to the surface as you are involved in creative, fulfilling, and satisfying days.

Possibilities for fulfilling creative work are everywhere, within everyone's reach— one must just learn to recognize and grasp them. The greatest potentials are often within the smallest things. The person who finds no pleasure in little events rarely finds pleasure in life's big occasions. It is not necessary to see the Pyrenees or the Himalayas to appreciate the wonders of nature—you can watch a butterfly emerge from its chrysalis in your kitchen window and witness one of nature's most spectacular sights. I am not suggesting that it wouldn't be wonderful to get to the Himalayas, but it's silly to sigh over the possibility so distractedly that you don't even see the garden spider or praying mantis you're stepping on.

It's not essential to have a fully equipped, picture-perfect studio, either. Beautiful work can emerge from the most chaotic sewing room. You start gradually, letting the work grow and develop. Many of the best-known fiber artists in this country started by having to clear the breakfast dishes away before they could sew on the kitchen table.

Learning to appreciate and enjoy the best in your surroundings and situation does not mean you will necessarily be completely satisfied with it. But you can at least exercise your capacities to enjoy all the positive aspects while attempting to change and improve the others.

This book offers a collection of ideas and proposals for accomplishing both personal and family goals. You are not required to desert your husband or abandon your children in order to be a whole, functioning, creative person. Getting-it-all-together-at-home is not easy. It is, as you'll read, worth all the energy, time, and effort that it inevitably requires.

In the chapters that follow many fiber artists are quoted directly. Some, anonymous by request, felt that the revelation of their true feelings would have serious repercussions at home, and a few thought their words would be grounds for divorce. Husbands are apparently unaware of the degree of dissatisfaction that some women feel. Thus, the writers of several deeply felt statements willingly shared their thoughts but preferred not to be identified. Still other unattributed comments are from women I met and talked with, but whose names I do not know.

My references to fiber artists vary according to their own preferences. Some asked to be referred to as craftsmen, some as craftswomen, others as craftspersons. I have tried to honor those requests, and thus the references are inconsistent. In my own writing, I have used "craftsman" to refer to any person involved in the crafts—and "craftswoman" when my reference was specifically directed to women in crafts. I am personally unresolved about "craftsperson." Many women have not resolved the matter of terms defining their roles, and while this may not be a crucial issue, it is a significant one. Once the roles are more clearly defined, selecting the terminology will be easier. Several women contacted me during the writing of this book to ask that their maiden names be added as middle names, or they reverted to them for professional use. Most women asked to be identified professionally as artists, teachers, writers, designers, authors, quilters, stitchers, or weavers. I have in initial reference to the fiber artists identified them briefly by their own descriptions: a fuller acknowledgment will be found at the end of the book.

"It takes a little madness and a lot of passion to spend as many hours working in the studio as I do. I couldn't live without it. But I couldn't live without my family either."

Jean Ray Laury (Photographer: Stan Bitters)

1.
Finding Time

"I *love* to make quilts and I love being a writer though I have days when I hate to write . . . of course it's difficult to juggle your schedule to get to do all the things you want to do but I haven't, for example, been bored since 1971."

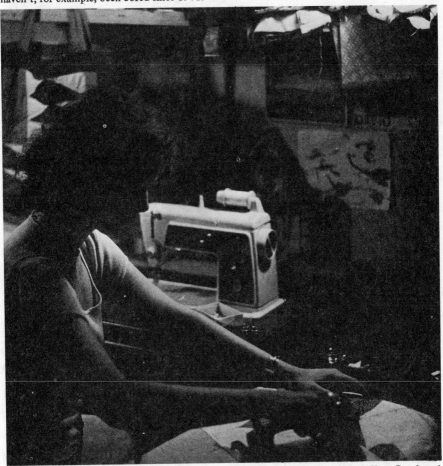

Beth Gutcheon (Photographer: Jeffrey Gutcheon)

There has always been time for the creative work because it's as necessary to my existence as eating. I would never have married a man who didn't understand that. My work has never taken anything away from the home—it has only enriched it. (K. Lee Manuel, exhibiting artist and teacher, California)

It's a struggle . . . I don't read anything but weaving books. I don't do volunteer work, my house is dirty, and I shop from the Sears catalog. We haven't done any social entertaining in years, but I find there is usually time to do most anything you want to badly enough. (Barbara Threefoot, weaver, New Orleans)

I do not recognize the 24-hour day. I did not invent it . . . it does not exist. (Robbie Fanning, author and publisher from California)

I take time to do my work well because it represents me. It is an integral part of my person-hood, in a way that cooking dinner is not. Many people who are basically not very interested in quilts tend to remark, 'My, that must take a lot of patience.' Well, of course it doesn't take patience if you like to do it—what takes patience, for me, is trying to remember what's in the refrigerator so I can think of what to have for dinner. That is demanding work, in my book. (Beth Gutcheon, quiltmaker and author)

I hear from all women about their frustrations with trying to fit in family with career. Something has to give, and usually it is the woman. (Norene Firth, writer, teacher, and artist)

•

Creative women, working at home, do not just "find" time for their work—they take it, carve it out of the day, plan for it. A serious fiber artist does not wait to see if there is an hour left over at the end of a day when the last dirty sock has been stuffed into the laundry basket, the dishes put away, and the counter scoured. Finding time may involve reshuffling some priorities, re-evaluating needs or re-educating the family. It requires stopping occasionally to take a critical look at the way time is spent.

It isn't necessary actually to neglect your home or ignore your family to devote yourself to your own work. Pressures vary of course—babies require more continuous care than ten-year-olds who are in school five or six hours a day. Schedules have to be adjusted according to needs. But don't ever lay your own work aside entirely, even in the busiest year. That's when it is most essential to continue with it.

It has never been difficult for me to find time for my work; my real difficulty has been in finding time to pick up a quart of milk or get the wet clothes into the drier or redeem the dry cleaning before the 30-day limit after which the management threatens to "dispose of all unclaimed articles." My own creative work always (almost always) gets done—plus whatever else can be sandwiched into the remaining time.

It has been my experience that when the demands on my time are the greatest, I'm most productive. Time becomes so valuable I don't waste any of it. When a commission is underway or when I'm very excited about a new quilt I'm designing, everything goes better. I am more efficient. Knowing how easily I can get totally involved in my work, I make a special effort to fix a casserole or dessert ahead of time. Five minutes of concentrated planning for nutritious and good-tasting meals is more productive than if I have all day in a kind of random and undirected activity.

Finding time is often a matter of finding your direction. Determine what it is you want to do and then it will be easier to accomplish that. Ask yourself if you want to create, produce, write, explore, exhibit, or invent. And ask if you are willing to work to do that.

I once spoke, along with four or five other fiber artists, at a textile conference. One of the other speakers, when asked to describe her role, said she was a wife, a mother, and an artist. I remember my surprise at hearing this since my answer would have been in reverse order—an artist, a mother, and a wife. We defined our roles differently, although we probably spent the same number of hours in the kitchen. How you view yourself varies of course with the ages of your children, your relationship to your partner, and your particular responsibilities at the time. But I have always thought of myself as an artist and writer. That established something crucial and basic for me. I added to this some other enriching and vital relationships (marriage, family, home) but they didn't change what I was. My needs as a person must come first. If they didn't, I think I might have been a poor mother. As it is, I feel good about the kind of mother I am and about my relationship with my children. Because I love my work I don't love my children less: it has given me a greater capacity to enjoy them and to encourage them in their own pursuits. If I'm not a whole person, how can I be a whole mother? My daughter does not see women or mothers as housekeepers. She has a more expanded view, and she knows that mothers write, lecture, and exhibit. I consider that an essential aspect of my being a good mother!

If I think of myself first as an artist that doesn't mean art always gets top priority. As an artist I can still spend the whole day playing Monopoly with a sick child or painting the dining room. My role as mother is listed second because of the dependence of children. Again, that's a variable determined by each child's age and ability to function independently. The time will come, I assume, when my children have left and the role of mother will be last on my list.

Men are presumed to be more self-sufficient, and so the role of wife can be third. Marriage is a sharing role, not one of dependence. As a wife you relate to another adult who is equally capable of fending for himself. I know some women whose art is most important, but who define their first role as that of "wife." It may be a peace-keeping device; it may be in deference to being supported, if her husband is a patron of her art! Very often it is just a matter of viewpoint—one's marriage is the most important relationship in life, but work may be the driving force. As artist and author Florence Pettit said, "He is first in my heart but my work is my life." Each is most important in a different way.

You might find that it helps clarify your view of your own roles to list them in order of their importance. In what order do you think your husband would list his roles?

You can be an artist *and* a good mother. Remember that a man can be an engineer or a dentist and it does not preclude his being a good father. Just as your husband can have a professional life as well as a home life, you can pursue your creative work in addition to being a homemaker.

It is interesting that marriage is often considered a full-time job for a woman, but *never* for a man. His career is furthered, not hindered, by marriage—this is not usually true for women. Fiber artists do assume they can have both—marriage *and* a career. And of course many of us *want* both—life doesn't seem complete if either is missing.

Erica Jong spoke eloquently of this in her article, "Daughters," in the *Ladies Home Journal*

Having had some of the fruits of success and fame . . . I am more than ever aware of the need for a personal life—for family, for children, for a man you can laugh with in the kitchen, read with in bed, and hug when either of you needs hugging.

One thing the phenomenon of "Fear of Flying" has done for me is to make me more and more aware of how empty life is when it is lived only in public—or only on paper. Of course, the life of a working writer is only "a sort of life" (as Graham Greene calls it) because so many hours are spent at the typewriter with imaginary people. But even so, one needs other things: a home, family and loving relationships. All people need both—the outer achievement and the inner life—but, unfortunately, while men have almost always been able to have both, women, alas, have had to choose.

For the woman who truly considers her role as wife and homemaker uppermost, there is no unrest. She has made a clear choice and willingly gives up other things to put that first. If she feels no frustration over that choice, she has no problem. The only difficulty is for those women who find the choice hard, or resent the fact that they must make a choice.

Oregon fiber artist Nancy Hoskins, the mother of four, wife of a doctor, and a graduate student in textiles, states:

Time is not found; it is created by a careful and thoughtful decision as to what one must do to maintain that delicate balance between you the individual with a strong inner sense of self-direction and you the multifaceted actress who plays wife, mother, artist, teacher, daughter, student, and friend. Essential to this balance is to recognize how important it is to you to have the time to grow and create; and then organize your time as best you can to accommodate to your desire.

I have gradually eliminated those activities that burned up time and energy with superfluous projects. Don't feel too guilty about all those community things . . . others are willing, and find great growth and satisfaction, where I only experience frustration and a sense of fragmentation. I am a "morning person" and my creative energies run high before noon, so I reserve my best hours for what I really want to do. By the time my family leaves each morning I am dressed, and the house is in reasonable order. I then mentally "leave" my hausfrau activities until my youngest returns. That is a beautiful unbroken stretch of hours . . . quiet and creative . . . I have been a full-time working wife and mother for half of my twenty years of marriage and believe me, being a humble housewife offers one of the world's most creative opportunities for personal growth and happiness if you use your gifts advantageously.

Diane Bower, a home economist, college teacher, spinner and quilter, wrote:

I have stopped doing the things I "ought" to do, such as PTA activities, volunteer projects, being a professional board member. Now I do what I have to do. For me this means working full time—which gives me the payoff I need financially, intellectually, and psychically. Doing what I have to do may mean writing a lecture, reading Fear of Flying, *or serving carry-out chicken because the flax flowers must be processed immediately for maximum dye extract.*

All needle arts are voracious consumers of time. And fiber artists all feel short-changed where time is concerned. Like money, time doesn't seem to go as far as it used to—the more things there are to spend it on, the less distance it covers. While each of us is given, daily, a new full period of 24 hours, the demands for that time vary and shift. It's a matter of how we choose to spend our 24 hours—what we exchange them for.

Personal relationships, everyone agrees, are what life is all about. And they do take time. A certain amount of time is also required in order to accomplish the day-to-day mechanics of living. These hours are relinquished a bit more grudgingly. Needs, responsibilities, and demands seem always to exceed the available time. That's when we must consciously select, choosing how we'll spend the limited hours, and this selection gives evidence to our priorities, whether or not they are consciously stated.

Women's roles vary according to personal needs and responsibilities: some work away from home for needed income, some care full time for small children, and some are committed to their art. Fiber artists hope to earn an income, care for children, *and* be creatively productive. Constant juggling and shifting are required to find a comfortable balance between the commitments to one's own work and to home and family. Sacrificing one's own work over a long period of time is frustrating and breeds resentment—one cannot function "out of balance" without creating tensions. Something wears thin.

Cathy Ryan, who works in a San Francisco art gallery, is single. She writes and does commissioned fiber work. This sounds glamorous and controlled to someone who spends hours daily driving children to nursery school, hauling the dog to the vet, getting kids to the orthodontist, and shopping and cooking for five. But Cathy says:

There really doesn't seem to be much balance. It's more a matter of the priority of the moment. If there is a deadline the housework suffers until the project gets done; or if friends drop in, the projects suffer. That just seems to be the way my life goes. It's never totally under control. I always seem to end up with too much to do and not enough time to do it.

That is a basic and seemingly universal problem for women, and few ever completely solve it. Maggie Turner, a stitcher from Portland, Oregon, puts it this way:

I don't find as much time as I would like as I feel guilty if I participate in my own creative endeavors when there are household chores that need to be done. I usually figure that after 9 p.m. the time is mine, but by then I'm usually too tired to do anything.

Jo Morris, who owns a quilt shop in New York, views her time this way:

I don't think I could ever "find time." I have 10 children, 3 to 23, with 7 boys left at home and a 13-room house. I just decided I would do it and make time for what was necessary. There are always some stumbling blocks. Sometimes it is necessary to shut down for a day or two and tend to the house and family. I work 30 to 35 hours a week on my business.

Each woman's program is different and relates to her own needs, as well as to the needs of her children and husband. Carole Austin, a California designer and soft-sculpture artist, has this view:

I have found that most of my problems I have created myself due to my background and my own feelings of guilt and lack of self-worth. My husband and I have spent many hours talking about my hangups, so to speak, and it really comes down to getting rid of that left-over guilt (that has no reason to be there) and taking care of some of my needs. The thing is that it really does not have to be at the cost of one's family which we are so brainwashed to believe.

Pat King, a stitchery artist from Houston, says:

Many of us who get things done have a large amount of energy and seem to be able to direct it in a creative way. Or is it that creating generates the energy? In any case I never sit around waiting for the Muse to tap me on the shoulder. There is always something going on in the workroom.

Enthusiasm also generates energy. If you awake eager and excited over a current project, you can accomplish essential household tasks in a shorter time. Some women find it helps to set time limits—by deciding that when the kids leave for school, they will go to their own studios. Some decide that what isn't finished at nine will be bluntly ignored. For me, that doesn't work. I'm more oriented to projects or goals than to time. I decide I'm going to complete something (writing an article or working out a particular design) and I *do* that. I don't stop to fix lunch or to call a friend or to water the plants until I finish. This is why I often like to work at night—it is open-ended. You never need to stop because of a meal or the phone.

Once you have determined what's important, that does not automatically solve things. Kids do get chicken pox four days before an exhibition deadline. Husbands bring last-minute guests home for dinner. In-laws arrive. Cars break down. There are always shifts and changes and one must remain flexible and receptive to them. (But then, kids do get invited to slumber parties, husbands go out of town on business, and the in-laws may invite everyone to *their* house for dinner.)

The way the day gets started is very important. I have always stayed in bed as long as possible (having been up too late the night before), but I like to get right at something in the morning. I almost always have breakfast with the children and then stagger right to my desk and do a little organizing, or sit down at the sewing machine and get started. Then I can stop and get dressed or make the bed and it is easy to go back to work. The direction for the day's activities is already set.

Beth Gutcheon accomplishes her work through a set schedule:

How I find time for what I do is the following. My son . . . goes to school at 9. I am home from taking him by 9:15 and I work until 2:45 when I have to pick him up. That means, I work. I don't meet anyone for lunch, I don't chat on the phone, I don't run out for the mail, I don't pick up a quart of milk. If I'm writing and the ideas won't come, then I sit there and stare at the blank page for five hours, but that is the time that I have so that is when I use it. None of this folderol about waiting for the Muse. Only a bachelor could have thought of a concept like that . . .

I do not find too much time for my house. I wash dishes when these is no more room in the sink for dirty ones, roughly every two days, and I try to do a massive cleanup, by which I mean having all the dirty laundry out of the living room, once a week . . . Jeffrey does his share willingly, *though I rarely remember to ask. I vacuum about once a week because I like to vacuum. The things I don't like, like washing floors and cleaning the bathroom, go for weeks, or until I'm expecting houseguests I don't know very well. I no longer straighten up before my mother-in-law comes. I discovered that cleaning up made me very angry, because I kept fuming to myself that the whole family had made the mess, but only I was worried about it and we can all see how unfair that is. Well, after a time I realized that I'd rather be happy than right, so I stopped worrying that there was a mess at all. And in fact it doesn't seem all that messy now. We're healthy and extremely neat about our persons and bathe every day, so I don't see what more is required.*

While your children are in school or your husband at work, you have your best opportunity to do the part of your own work that requires the most concentration. Don't squander that valuable time on household tasks. Less demanding parts of your work can be done later in the day amidst activity. Fold the laundry while you talk (and don't be selfish or self-sacrificing—be willing to share those tasks).

How you start work in the morning and how you arrange the work schedule are really matters of technique. The essential thing is determining what is important. Finding the time is a second step: what you are finding the time *for* is the crucial element. What do you really want to do? Who are you? What do you want to be? Decide. Write it down. Face up to it and then do something about it.

One well-known stitchery artist and designer describes it this way:

It seems to me that the whole thing is a problem of definition: women deciding who they are and how they want to go about being that. When young people ask me about doing both (career and home/family) I advise them to get a really good start on their work and themselves before they get into marriage. I had neither. The change was difficult for everyone to handle.

Regarding time, she added:

The key to "finding time" for work and home lies in how one sees oneself. I see myself more as a working artist who also happens to be a mother and a "former-wife." My daughters always participated in my work, giving me ideas, helping me, and generally enjoying the way it has enlarged their lives. When I was married, my husband had similar attitudes, up to a point. Obviously, I exceeded his limits.

Designer, quilter, and author Jody House has written clearly on this facet of the problem of time:

I do not find time to do all that needs to be done, I make the time by constantly setting priorities. I try to look at what is important to me, what is important to the people with whom I live, and attempt to find some balance so that everyone is able to have some of their most important "wants."...

I think that what it all boils down to is how you value yourself, therefore your time and efforts. . . . Many women with whom I come in contact seem to live their lives through others . . . never committing themselves to the scary idea of putting their own values and opinions on the line. Some wake to this realization and are able to develop, some never quite get around to getting it all together. It is my impression when I see a student of mine unable to decide, without the help of her decorator, what color yarn to choose for the sampler pillow, that this inability to make decisions shows a lack of control over her own life.

It is very easy to assume the role of "housewife" and to be provided for, have someone else make the major decisions, confine yourself to caring for your family. Unfortunately, most of us need to care for ourselves also. I think that every individual needs to grow, if you do not grow and change with and through living, one day you will turn around and find that every-

one around you has grown–gone–from you and you cannot understand why. I think that it is important to make a commitment to yourself, choose something that you want to do or to learn about, and poke your head out of the warmth and security of the nest and take a chance on yourself. A little success can work wonders!

Teacher and fiber craftsman Jane Chapman views herself in her professional role. While she never had small children ("ours came partly grown"), she did have home responsibilities:

I never think about finding time for both work and home. Work is and always has been part of life and I consider them together. Everyone juggles time to take in what is important. I gradually gave up the nonessentials (to me) like a good bit of social life, canvassing, PTA meetings, yes, even art exhibits (unfortunately, many of those are only important to those who are in them) to have the time for what is important to me. Fortunately as you mature and grow, you are able to see what's important more clearly and there is less struggle to make up your mind. Also you have to enjoy what you are doing–and I don't mean just the gravy part but the nitty gritty too. I enjoy having a well-organized house and life and the few hours a week it takes are well worth it. If you never get hopelessly behind on "maintenance-type" things about your life you can save yourself a lot of worry and guilt feelings (or whatever it does to you) and such feelings can take a lot out of your creative life.

If you are in the midst of the middle-class four-in-a-family, and wife-in-the-kitchen setup, take advantage of what it has to offer. Who besides the homemaker has so much control over her own time and her own day?

Economics usually require that someone in a household earn the necessary income for family needs. Children need someone to attend to and care for them, particularly for the first five years. Certain mechanics are essential in any living arrangement. Whether you live in a bachelor apartment, a three-generation household, or a commune, food is consumed, groceries purchased, beds are slept in, garbage gets taken out, and dirty clothes accumulate. Dirty dishes and laundry are not the exclusive possessions of wives and mothers. Anyone who eats from dishes has dishes to be washed. Even the most handsome bachelor or glamorous girl in the singles apartment probably owns a vacuum cleaner and a dish cloth. So get the mechanics of living out of the way. If you don't enjoy them, at least be efficient enough so that they won't interfere. I have learned to tolerate housework. It's a different pace and allows thinking time.

Husbands and children willingly assume their share of tasks if they understand that your work matters. It's only when they feel that "mother isn't doing anything important anyway" that they take advantage. You don't question the value of what they do; they should reciprocate. Share with them, talk about your work. You may find they will enjoy helping you. (You may also find that they are reluctant to give up their full-time maid, dietician, chef, waitress, bottle-washer, chauffeur, valet, and cleaning service, and that will take some time to remedy. If I had someone to do that for me, I'd resist change too!)

My sister, writer Jackie Vermeer, had these comments about finding time for homemaking:

I don't always find time for all my work. It becomes a matter of not making a clean house one of my top priorities. The family doesn't even notice if the floor hasn't been mopped and waxed, or if the dishes haven't all been washed. :

Sometimes I work only on my project (taking time out to fix meals and to see that everyone has a few clean clothes) for as many days as I can. Then I take one whole day and catch up on the housework. What doesn't get done that day will have to wait.

Other times I will just use my work as a reward. Like do a certain number of household chores, and then the rest of the day is mine. With this method I can really get a lot done in a hurry.

The scheduling of time for fiber work and for home is open to a great variety of approaches. Peggy Moulton, stitcher from California, says:

I find time by having an organized routine and doing only the essentials in housework (and lowering my standards, too). I clean one room a day. The whole house is seldom clean at once, but conversely, it's seldom shot to hell at once either. . . .

One must educate one's family. Let them know that you aren't going to do all their little chores for them.

Joan Michaels-Paque, a Wisconsin fiber artist, teacher and author, writes:

I have long since learned not to procrastinate. I seem to accomplish more when things are neat and clean. Don't waste time searching for things. I frequently make priority lists. Also, to be honest, I expect a great deal from my family, but not more than I am willing to do myself.

Most fiber artists find some degree of frustration or conflict in trying to resolve the problems of time. Shirley Fink, who describes herself as a weaver, teacher, wife, mother, friend, and person, said about her scheduling:

Before teaching full time at Boston University, there was minimal problem finding time for work, as that was all I did—work on my work full time. Now that I have so full a teaching commitment, I find myself very frustrated about the time problem; I am in the process of trying to find a more satisfactory solution.

My husband and I are both unconcerned about dust and clean windows—our children have acquired our slovenly habits by osmosis (except when the younger one chooses to rebel and cleans her room).

Gayle M. Feller, California artist, teacher, and craftsperson comments:

I find it extremely difficult to find time for my art work as well as time to take care of my home. Since I am a widow with three teenaged children I find myself going completely mad at times. Teaching both children's and adult classes keeps me at the gallery from 9 to 3. I do other work there at the gallery as well and my schedule is gruelling at times. My own creative efforts must take place in the evening or on the weekends. If I have an idea that really needs to be "spit out" immediately, I find myself feeling such pressure that I get up and work during the night.

Betty Friedan, in *The Feminine Mystique*, describes how Parkinson's Law functions in terms of housework. Housekeeping tasks always seem to expand to fill all the available time. If you have thirty minutes available, they require thirty minutes; if you have eight hours, housework magically swells and consumes eight hours. Her theory was very helpful to me in learning to budget my time.

Another stitcher adds that she doesn't feel that being female makes her more qualified than others to do cleaning chores. "I'm constantly saying, 'I'm not the maid.'"

Linda Cross, author and craftswoman from New York, says:

I worked in my studio full time, painting and doing free-lance craft designing for years before our child was born. Since then I've continued my work, but it hasn't been easy.

Frankly, I'm really looking forward to reading about how others solve these problems. Some days I plod along, not doing any of my jobs well, feeling that I'm trying to do too much, at least while my child is small and needs constant attention. Then, on other days everything seems to work together: my son and I baking bread together, an organized household, and my work coming along in a very fruitful, happy way.

Elsa Brown, a Connecticut artist and author, adds:

I keep fairly regular working hours just as someone going to the office. We all "pick away" at household chores. The children have always done their own as well as the household laundry. My husband does the grocery shopping from a list that I prepare.

Some artists have resorted to very unconventional but workable schedules to accommodate their needs. One friend of mine who frequently works all night on her art told me that her neighbors thought she was pretty odd. "Of course," she added, "I think it's pretty odd and rather dull if someone never gets excited enough about their work to stay up all night."

Another fiber artist who works at night, Nancy Lipe, writes:

MiAe and I keep strange hours to avoid interruptions. Bedtime 6 a.m. Get up time 2 p.m. We avoid a lot of telephone calls that way, usually it's just the answering service for Dew, anyway. So we don't miss anything but the interruption. Also we have no wall phone. Everything on a jack which we pull before going to bed or when casting resin, dying fabric, or painting with quick-dry paint.

According to Ilene Ferrini-Tuttle, painter and exhibiting tapestry designer from California, the way to solve the time problem is:

Organize, organize, organize. Organize the chaos! Strive to keep a routine for the family and a routine for yourself in between and after. I burned a lot of late night oil and never knew what "natural light" was until my children were in school! These things worked for me:

1) I couldn't stand a messy looking home—even though it wasn't spotless—so if I couldn't keep up with the dust I became very frustrated. Finally, I hired a cleaning woman one day a week and my whole life changed. It was an extravagance for us, but I sacrificed everything I could to manage it; it was my liberation from one of the stumbling blocks to free time.

2) Wall-to-wall carpeting (even reed-mat type) hides dust.

3) Develop a good list of quick dinner menus.

4) Find good day-care centers.

Says Ricky Clark, quiltmaker and stitcher from Oberlin, Ohio:

I find that every time someone calls to ask if I can do something in the community (which happens almost daily) I quickly review my schedule, eliminate the time I was planning to work on this piece of stitchery and say "yes." Now that I see this happening I'm able to be tough about it. This piece is extremely important to me, and I don't want to keep sacrificing it. Community good works are important, too, so I have to make decisions. . . . For me being arbitrary is the answer.

Robbie Fanning offers this on how she manages her time:

I run two-three miles a day to have the energy to run on 98% efficiency. No TV. Generally no car (bicycle). One child by quite deliberate choice. Get up at 5:30 a.m. Good sense of humor. Love to sleep, dream. Love to read. Take phone off the hook. Jump in bed readily. Plug away at things little by little, rather than waiting till I have to move mountains to accomplish anything. Try to set realistic goals. An inveterate listmaker. Try to listen to my body's rhythms and not fight them. Am not a compulsive neat. Love myself.

Unfinished projects are a subject of concern to many artists. Paula Foster, artist from Davis, California, says:

A sense of direction and pride make me finish every project even if it turns out I don't like it when it is done. I still work through it. I don't like to see anything undone. It's like leaving a part of my life dangling.

Cam Smith Solari, author and photographer, adds:

Incomplete cycles are very hard on people. Having things half-finished and lying around can make a person feel tired and unhappy. Attention gets stuck on those incomplete cycles of action. Finishing projects, answering mail, finishing the hem, picking up the papers, whatever . . . makes a person feel good and ready to do new things. So if I'm not being as productive as I want to be and things aren't going quite right, I make a list of all the incomplete cycles I have (even very minor ones) and I finish them . . . and then I have a lot more energy and it is easier to work.

For housework and related activities we have a blue dot board. Since we both work, my husband and I share household chores. We agreed what things we wanted to be responsible for. I do the housecleaning, cooking, and laundry and he does repairs, bill paying, lawn watering, and buys the food and takes care of the plants. Each specific chore is written on a board and every week we fill in a blue dot if the chore was done.

We don't discuss whether the chores are done or not. If they don't get done, they don't get done. Creative projects definitely come first. I love the blue dot board because it makes what I have to do in the house very specific and I don't have the feeling that I ought to be cleaning. . . .

I have to laugh a little trying to communicate about the blue dot board. I'm afraid people would look a little strangely at somebody who gives themselves dots for doing housework. All I know is that it gives me some control over an area that tends to have no beginning and no ending . . . the ever-present blur of housework. It really allows me to take my attention off the house, and still feel I'm doing my domestic duty. I do feel better and I work better when my environment is clean and tidy . . . and pretty.

June Steinbaugh, a weaver and partner in Weavers Workshop in New Orleans, made this statement:

A luxurious day to me is to get up in the morning, have breakfast with the family and as soon as everyone is off to school and the office I go from the breakfast table in my robe to the loom and start weaving—several hours or all day. On these days I accomplish a lot.

If I finish breakfast and start straightening up the kitchen, inevitably the phone rings and while I am talking on the phone I see the grocery list, the fingerprints on the wall or the dust on the shelves. After the phone call, I shower and find that I have run out of clean clothes and so my day is planned—run to the grocery, clean the fingerprints off the wall, dust the shelves, run the washing machine, and before you know it the kids are home from school.

We all need to stop occasionally and take a good long look at how we are using our days. Select what's most important and put it first. Many women feel trapped and assume they have no choices, when they actually do. I've heard, often, "I love to read but I just don't have time for it anymore." This same person may sunbathe daily or play bridge twice a week. There is nothing wrong with getting a tan or with playing bridge—but be careful not to kid yourself. If you play bridge and don't read, admit that you prefer bridge. Don't pretend to prefer one thing (or even to suffer over the lack of it) while actively choosing another.

Actually, what each of us would really like to have is the equivalent of a wife. I'd like someone who would take care of my clothes, mend, sew, plan meals, buy groceries, organize the refrigerator, attend PTA, cook, bake, invite friends over, plan and prepare for entertaining, write the thank-you notes after Christmas, do the shopping, run the laundry through, fold the towels, remember my birthday and my favorite recipes, respond to my moods, cater to my whims and needs, take my children to the dentist, put in two hours at the co-op nursery, vacuum, clean the sinks and toilets, sweep occasionally, wash the windows, water the plants, answer the phone, gracefully decline most invitations, and who would be grateful if I "let" her have an outside job.

That would leave me time to putter in the garden, read to the children, read to myself, attend social or educational functions, take care of myself and allow for my full-time commitment to my teaching, designing, or writing.

Even without wives, if writing or a craft is important to you, there is time for it. There may not be time for *all* the things you want to do, though; you have to decide what is most important and set your priorities. But these aren't permanent— they may change from week to week, or from one season to the next. They will certainly change from year to year—and dramatically change your life!

But you must decide what it is that you want to do and then *do* it. No excuses. Make the most of whatever situation is yours. Change it where you can, and where you can't, take advantage of it.

Finding time for work is arranging your priorities. You have to know what is important to you and what is not. You have to limit your social life, we find. It means none, except business-related, during the week, some on weekends when you're not too tired or when the house is in order. Casual get-togethers with warm friends become more numerous. (Marilyn Heise, editor and publisher of The Working Craftsman*)*

I notice that time is the last thing I compute when figuring a job, a hangover from the house-wife syndrome, in which a woman is unable to see any tangible results of her work. (Carol Cheney Rome, author of needlepoint books)

Set a schedule—for me it's 10 to 4:30. Do the housework weekends. That way if you want to have fun weekends, all you skip is the housework. I beg, borrow or maneuver all the work out of other people I possible can. (Catherine Gibson, California artist)

I feel extremely lucky to have work like that to do. When Jeffrey and I were first married, he left architecture and moved to New York to live in one room and fail to become a rock and roll star. (He plays the piano.) Actually, he did more or less become a rock and roll star after a few years but in the beginning none of our friends or relations could understand what we were doing at all, living on beans and trying to write and play the piano, for heaven's sake. But once in a while, some childhood beau of mine would take Jeffrey aside and say, "You know, I've always thought that it would be great to leave Wall Street for a year and just do whatever I want to do most. I envy you," and when J. asked why he didn't just do it, he would answer, "Because there was never anything I wanted to do that much."

I love to make quilts, and I love being a writer, though I have days when I hate to write, as I'm sure you do too. Of course it's difficult to juggle your schedule to get to do all the things you want to do, but I haven't for example, been bored since 1971. I'm really grateful for that, and I'd rather have all the scheduling problems in the world and go to bed every night with things still hanging that I really want to get to, than not have "anything I wanted to do that much." (Beth Gutcheon)

"I know that I'm only really happy when I'm working so it is always difficult to have to stop."

Constance Howard (Photograph courtesy of West London Observer)

2.
Finding Space

"Training friends to see you as a serious working artist, whose time cannot be taken over with koffee klatches, volunteer work, meetings, and telephone chats, is very important."

Elsbeth Ramos (Photographer: R. Carofano)

The space for my work is taken from our ten-room apartment in New York. How much of it, you might ask—the answer is all of it, except for the two children's bedrooms (although they are also invaded during the summer when the family is away). (Erica Wilson, teacher, designer, and author of books on needlecraft)

I have always dreamed of having a separate, fully equipped studio—well designed and organized, with everything at hand. But for now, I make do with a corner of my bedroom. I have a large table, an old dental chest with lots of drawers, a smaller table for my jigsaw, and tons of sawdust all over everything. (Sally Wetherby, craftswoman, California)

We don't have storage space, do have interruptions, do have messes—a lot of activity around here. Mainly, though, we have a much more satisfying life-style than most—which as a woman, I have crafts to thank for. (Nancy Wettlaufer, potter and writer)

I've decided that a studio is a state of mind and I'd get nothing done if I made everything tidy first. Given that the average American housewife wakes up in an unmade bed, she gets off to an unpromising start for the day. (Ann deWitt, California craftswoman)

To store things I stuff things in closets, kick bags under the window seats and have finished things where the window curtains ought to be. (Ann La Pietra, toymaker and owner of The Kids' Place, Illinois)

●

The first time you decide to leave the sewing machine up or your work out, you have started your studio. Another giant growth spurt occurs when you decide one night to have dinner in the kitchen or on trays because the dining room table is covered with a current project. The studio expands like a creature out of science fiction, moving silently but tenaciously from one shelf to the next, devouring all available space. Areas once acquired are seldom relinquished.

So the studio mushrooms in the midst of household chaos and activity. In fact, the more chaotic or active the household, the greater the need for a studio. (A quiet, peaceful house probably has quiet areas all ready to move into, not requiring a forklift or a show of force to establish residence.) It is when you finally outgrow the end of the dining room table or overflow from the family room into the kitchen that you start thinking of a planned studio.

A place to work, a special space, is crucial. Without it, hours can be spent dragging out materials and putting them away, using up time and energy in nonproductive activity. The choice about whether that studio area is best at home or away from home is (for the beginner) often a purely rhetorical question. The need is for space—anywhere. Perhaps only those women who have already achieved some degree of financial success are likely to have the luxury of choice among adding a new room, revamping an existing one, or renting a studio.

Most of us start out working at home because it is *possible* in fibers and fabrics to have a working space in conjunction with living arrangements. We also start out at home because there are no paying jobs in the fiber arts field for beginners—especially not if you want to do personal, expressive work. Free-lance work is by far the most common direction, and for that you must provide your own working space.

So studios must grow where they can. Sewing machines plant themselves firmly on dining room tables, photographic developing trays in laundry rooms and bathrooms, and pottery wheels in patios and garages; typewriters root like weeds, waiting to take over the next available table space; and few guest rooms or closets are safe from encroaching yarns and fabrics. Work where you can; take advantage of whatever situation presents itself.

One distinct advantage of the home studio is that it is not costly. It means simply adapting what is already available, at least to start with. Actually, carving out the studio space is not the problem—it's more a matter of trying to retain an area for other aspects of living. When both the fiber artist and her partner are involved in creative work, or when there is a philosophic agreement between them on the validity and importance of the creative work, space is no problem. Very often the life-style is such that living and working are synonymous, and any divisions are somewhat arbitrary. One's work has greater significance than any particular meal, so the dining room table is fair game for a project.

It is when another member of the family sets great store by a magazine-perfect formal living room, and envisions you as the perfect housekeeper, that conflicts tend to arise. (Obsessions with tidiness are easy to nurture if someone else is doing the tidying up.) Some women have found that separate studios are best because they help to avoid these conflicts. The garret has given way to the garage, which makes an excellent studio if there is a way to heat it in winter. Separate buildings are sometimes available for remodeling—other artists have studios built adjacent to the house. Still others rent space away from home. But whatever the nature of the studio, the important thing is having space available for work. That legitimizes the activity and recognizes its importance. As Diane Bower says, "The family room has been converted to a studio. By simply renaming and reorganizing the same room, I feel my work has become increasingly professional." Lynda Lanker, painter and textile artist adds, "My studio is a very small one, and all my painting and drawing and stitchery are jammed together in this tiny unkempt place. But it is *mine*, and it's a place to work, which is something a lot of people don't have."

Among those artists who prefer to work away from home, several found that shared studio space was a good answer. It cuts costs, allows for larger facilities, and offers an opportunity to exchange thoughts and ideas with other people professionally involved in art.

Ilene Ferrini-Tuttle says this regarding her studios at home and away:

Working at home was never satisfactory for me, but I did, of necessity, do so for many years—usually with space in the garage during the day, and in the kitchen at night. Also, taking classes gave me studio space away from home. As soon as it was feasible I took a working studio away from home in an old cannery, which fortunately is very cheap and adequate. This has another advantage for me because from time to time I've asked other artists to share my space and I find this stimulating.

24

Carol Cheney Rome writes:

I had to work in our townhouse at first, which was a disaster, creating tension and mess and inviting curious cats to rummage in their favorite commodities. Another insidious feature of having your work right in the house is that the work day can stretch and stretch. I found that I could use my work as an excuse for not relating to my family in the evenings and at other times, and it was difficult knowing that all those Unfinished Projects were right there just waiting for attention.

I have since rented rooms in an office building and moved everything into what is called, by my friends, The Warehouse. I feel no compunctions about closing the door on a god-awful mess, and no one has the prerogative to blast me for making messes. Makes me feel more "professional," having an office address and office phone.

A great advantage to having a studio or a work area, regardless of where it's located, is what it does to your attitude about your work. It helps define your role. Having the separate room or space gives you a "set" about work. You know that when you enter that room, it's to work. You don't make out the grocery list or hem a skirt there. Psychologically you prepare yourself—your mental framework can be attuned so that once you are in the room (or sit down at your end of the dining table) you're ready to go. It doesn't mean you can't work elsewhere as well; it simply means that specific area is only for the pursuit of your work. It's like "going to the office"—a work space devoted to your materials. It offers a reference point to your work.

Helen Bitar, artist-craftsman from Oregon, comments:

I never had to have a separate studio . . . I learned to work in my home because I like being at home—it is cozy and warm and comfortable. But because I have chosen home it also has had to be a place where I can live peacefully and part of the peace is having everything in its order so when I am working I usually keep my materials in a very small place where I can come and go to work and still feel comfortable about being in the room not having messes all over the room. Once in a while when I am doing something very large I will have to use the whole room and will accomplish putting the thing together in some form in a few days so the room is once more back at peace.

If you are short of space, if you have no studio and there is no place where your own art or craft may be pursued, perhaps you need to make a different *use* of your home. A "room of one's own," about which Virginia Woolf wrote so stirringly, is essential.

A house tends to take over. It can dictate the way you live if you let it. You must decide that you are its master, not its mistress. The house should be flexible, ready to give, alter, or adjust to the changing needs of you and your family. Too many people become victims of the structures in which they live. Walls are left bare, rather than covered with children's drawings, photographs, or paintings—from fear of a nail hole. I have seen women let the cost of their carpet be the deciding factor in how they used a space. It sounds absurd, yet some people allow their furnishings to dictate how they live their lives. They build a stage set and then find they must perform the appropriate leading role.

It is crucial to decide who is in charge—you or your house. Many women have lamented to me that they longed to weave but had no space for a loom. Or they wanted to quilt and had no room to spread out their fabrics. Or they wanted to write but had no place for quiet, to concentrate and pursue the writing. Yet almost every one had a living room, largely unused; a formal dining room, rarely used; and a large bedroom, half empty.

Granted, a forceful creative urge will find its way out. A determined person can work anywhere. If you are one of the vital artistic forces of the twentieth century, your work will surface. But how about the tentative, untried, unsure creative urge? If you're not a Mariska Karasz or an Anni Albers, then you need all the assistance a good physical setup can provide.

Why *not* put your loom in the living room? (Only one weaver said her husband complained, when he could no longer see the football game through the warp.) Why *can't* you sew in the living room, or paint there, or write at the dining room table? *You* make the rules in your house.

Creative work in progress fascinates guests of all ages. Your friends will love you no less if you let your stitchery supplant a coffee table full of magazines and ash-trays. In some houses, the possibility that a stranger might arrive at the front door provides the absurd justification for keeping the room pristine and unused.

Many homes allow special areas for children's play, for game rooms, for laundry, for a husband's den or study, for guests, and even for storage—but no room for the woman who needs space for her own work, an area that may be essential to help her find her own identity, or peace, or creative direction, or equilibrium. Or sanity.

Simple mechanics can alter the way you work. The driving force in creative work ought to be philosophic or aesthetic—sometimes, surprisingly, it's merely physical. Having a desk has (in a minor way) changed my life. It is a real office desk with drawers and compartments and knee-space. At first I thought it was really a bit ostentatious—after all, my first books were written with stacks of manila folders, boxes of notes, rainbows of papers stacked around me on the floor, mountains of carbons and the typewriter on the dining room table. This will, obviously, work. But having a desk simplifies many of the humdrum mechanical and practical aspects of the work. Everything came within reach. I didn't have to interrupt my thinking or writing to find an eraser or search for the dictionary, or get a new sheet of paper. Everything was at hand, in a designated place. It organized the mechanics of writing.

If you can't get a desk, lay siege to a drawer in the kitchen. Keep your tablets or sketch pads, pencils and pens at hand—within a second's reach. But allow your-self the essential luxury of a place to collect the materials necessary to your craft. Jody House applied this idea to her whole family:

We have tried to create personal space for each family member. Even if it is one drawer, one shelf or table. Other family members respect this privacy. I don't think that you can expect to have your things left alone (respected) by others if you do not do the same for them. I try not to overflow too much in my need for space. Fortunately, the needlework that I do is not very messy nor does it require lots of equipment. (This may be one reason that I chose to work in this area.)

For years I worked on the dining room or kitchen table, always putting away either dishes or sewing. Extra shelves and cupboards eased the storage, and to pro-vide more table space, I placed a four-by-eight-foot sheet of plywood, covered with Naugahyde, over a smaller table to get a temporary large work surface. When not in use it could be set up against the wall. (But what would you do with all the stuff on the table!) Two sheets of plywood, joined by a piano hinge, made a huge work surface to go over a large work table.

The sewing machine occupied the living room along with my large work table. The typewriter was in the dining room. Sewing was everywhere, except in the bedroom where my husband had work space. I was orderly, most of the time. My husband had an office and work area at the University at that time, my children had their own rooms, tree-houses, and desks at school. So it seemed perfectly natural to all of us that I have space too.

Now I enjoy the luxury of my own studio, full of light, cupboards, storage space, and wall displays. It's great to have the space. It doesn't mean one is confined to it, but it does make it off-limits for other activities.

My present studio (adjacent to the kitchen and with a deck going outdoors) has a desk, files, lots of cupboards, drawers, storage, a big work table, sewing machine, light table, fireplace and closets. I love the room and I am *very* protective of it—nobody can gain squatters' rights to any portion of it.

I like a well-ordered work area. My husband, a sculptor, also has his studio at home in what looks to me like total chaos. His desk and several workrooms are all chaotic. That's fine for him since it seems to work. But I don't want *my* studio like that. Eternal vigilance is the price. I must protect my studio, because naturally, when he and the kids run out of table space, a cleared table in my studio looks pretty inviting. We share a graphics area where drawings, slides, and drafting materials are kept. It's not always easy for me since I clean up right after I finish a job—and he never cleans up until he is ready to start a new one. We try to respect one another's ways of working and each other's work areas.

I fold and stack fabrics out where I can see them, on open shelves. Having the material visually available is important to me. But I also stick some things in drawers because it's nice to "discover" them later. The floor gets stacked with quilts, fabrics, boxes, and baskets. But my work areas I like open—the work table and counter tops, ready for a new project. Storage is essential. When I'm ready to work, excited about a new idea or design, I don't want to shop for materials. I want to work. I prefer to collect in advance the materials that appeal to me—then when I'm working on an idea I choose from what I have available.

Ann deWitt finds standard soda pop or beer can boxes good for fabric. Cut in half (as they usually are at the grocery store) they are just the right size to hold folded fabrics side by side, so that every color can be seen. Many women find ice-cream cartons (the big round three-gallon size) excellent inexpensive storage. They can be stacked on their sides so the contents are visible. Plastic bags are used by many fiber artists who remark on the importance of seeing their materials.

If creative activity is important for your own pleasure, well-being, and sanity, then you must obtain the space for it. If friends or family are offended to find your work in the living room, perhaps their real objection is to something within you (or themselves). You are not your living room! Think twice before you invite the offended person again, but it may be difficult to keep anyone away—a household full of activity and creative projects is very inviting. Almost anyone with a spark of the inquisitive or adventurous will want to be in such a home.

Every home has room for some crafts activities, since many require only limited space. Kitchens adapt readily to studio use. The fountain at San Francisco's Hyatt Hotel on Union Square originated in a kitchen studio. The sculpture was formed from bread dough by Ruth Asawa and her friends, neighbors, and family. The figures were cast in bronze for permanent installation. Other women, casting candles on the back porch or silkscreening on the kitchen table, have expanded their interests into full-time businesses.

To some extent, you have to plan your projects according to available space, but there are always ways of accomplishing large works if you are determined and flexible. In good weather, and in good climates, the outdoors offers almost limitless space. Porches, basements, garages, extra bedrooms, bedrooms in use (not extra), the kitchen—any space is usable. Nothing is sacred. Certainly not in Peggy Ritsi's house! This teacher and shop owner from California dominates "70% of the house. I'd be more spread out but I feel that bathrooms are not accomodating, nor are my two children's bedrooms."

Karen Jahncke, designer and doll maker, found a bedroom studio very workable:

I am rather ashamed to say that the Factory, as we call it, has taken over the master bedroom in our house. We have a very small house, and are bursting at the seams. I used to work in a dressing room/nursery. But between babies and cramped quarters, I greedily looked for more space. I rationalized the Great Bedroom Takeover by explaining that we go to bed late and wake up early; we spend such a little amount of time in the bedroom whereas I spent six to eight hours daily in the Closet/Factory. So it was generously agreed to squeeze the bed into the small room, and the Factory just burst into full bloom in the bedroom.

Storage is a continuing challenge for most people working with fibers. Some like everything visually available; others prefer to put everything away and bring it out of hiding when new projects are started. Helen Bitar says:

I store my materials in trunks and closets . . . instead of having everything around where I can see the stuff. If I had it around I would no longer see what I had to work with . . . it would become just part of the room. It is always refreshing to start a new project and then "get the stuff out" that I am going to work with and be very excited about the materials.

Stitcher Carole Clark finds cardboard file boxes indispensable. Organized files hold all design ideas, references, magazine articles, catalogs, and information for her teaching. One huge file contains all the miscellaneous.

Joan Michaels-Paque stores work

in every nook and cranny. Am in the process of finishing an upstairs studio. One section has a slanted roof where the ceiling will be covered with removable dowels filled with cones of yarn. In essence a fiber sky. One need only to glance up to see what's available and then pull out cord to measure what is needed.

Most fiber artists want a studio desperately if they don't have one. And they revel in the joy of their own private space when they do. For instance, Carole Austin says:

When we remodeled our garage into a family room and bath, I drew up the plans and included a workroom for myself which I share with the laundry facilities. My family and I call it my "ivory tower" because I love that room so much. I cannot tell you the feeling of joy at having my own private work space. I practically live there and it has a door that I can close! All the

28

years before this I had a card table set up in some room, usually our bedroom which I felt always had to be picked up. . . .

Bonnie Bartell, exhibiting artist from Oregon, says:

For many years I managed to mess up about every room in the house with my projects. I finally got a small studio . . . we have a new house with a studio designed into it for each of us.

And Robbie Fanning writes:

I have always had a desk and have always wished for a larger one. My husband built himself a beautiful teak desk and I immediately moved in, like a marauding bandit. He then bought a large desk when Saturday Review *went out of business. Guess where I'm writing this?*

Jackie Vermeer takes space

wherever I can find it. Before I had a real work table I used my desk until it got too crowded and then I'd take over the dining table. Everyone else has outside space for their work—the kids have their desks at school, Lou has his desk at the office. My home is my office, so obviously I need more space than they do. When you work at home, you must assume that you have a right to your own private work space—if you don't, you won't get it. Certainly no one is going to offer it to you.

Crafts designer and fiber artist Jerrie Peters offers this regarding her ability to devour space:

Bob paneled in our two-car garage to make a studio for me and this worked completely for a short period of time. Then, when it became evident that certain media didn't mix, such as wood and fiber, projects started finding their way back on the dining room table, the kitchen table, the family room, etc. Now we have added onto the house, plus a separate small workshop for wood work. In addition to this there are two project areas in the house and the children have work spaces designed to their particular interests in their rooms. At the moment this is working beautifully and dining, living, kitchen and master bedrooms are free of all projects with the exception of the unfolded laundry. (Back to the drawing board.)

We live in a large older house, with one extra room. Of course, when we moved here five years ago, that room would be my husband's study. Some day he would write there!! By the time he got home from work he did little writing, so slowly but surely with the help of my father I moved into the empty room. We covered the walls with shelves and fabric is stored color coded around the walls. I still use my husband's huge desk as my sewing table, but this is now my studio and I leave the iron up, the sewing machine out and I clean it up when I damn well please. (Rose Dwight, quiltmaker and quilting teacher from Ohio)

My work is so much a part of my (our) life-style that there is no storage problem. Yarn is on display in the living-room-showroom in baskets and bowls as are natural materials in crocks, vases and so forth. The finished goods literally cover the walls. (Patricia Foley, fiber designer, Oregon)

I use the living room for my studio though it continues to function as the living room at the same time. (Momo Nagano, weaver, California)

I live in an old (but cozy) one room cabin in the country and all the space except for my bed is taken up for working—two long tables for cutting, sewing, ironing, etc. Two entire walls are lined with shelves to store my fabrics (arranged by color). (Barbara Neill, fabric artist and craftsman from Oregon)

Sewing happens all over the house. It's a large old house. We traded working plumbing, etc. for space. I store things in the bottom half of every closet in the house, on the walls, in the basement and attic. Every time another of the four kids goes off to college, I get another room. (Mary Sprague, artist and teacher from St. Louis)

We made the dining room my work room, and moved the dining room things to the living room. It is a little bit of extra work to carry all the food to the living room to eat, but certainly worth it to have my work space. The extra bedroom is my husband's work room. I also needed a darkroom so we made the small laundry room into my darkroom. Our nice washing machine is stored in the cellar where it can't get used, and I have to take clothes to the laundromat, but again it is a matter of deciding what is more important and I had to have a darkroom, even if there wasn't space for it. (Cam Smith Solari)

I store materials in brown paper bags. I can tell what's in each by the way it's crumpled. The closet is filled with brown paper bags and bags are stuffed behind the bed, each with its very own special crumples. (Yvette Woods, exhibiting artist and teacher)

"I'm now putting my works on the ceiling because all the walls are full."

Yvette Woods (Photographer: Sam Wayne)

30

3.
On Being Superwoman

"It all began when I had two babies close together and decided there had to be more to life than wiping bottoms and washing diapers. Writing seemed like the logical answer—something that could be done at home and marketed through the mails. What began as a simple creative outlet has developed into an all-consuming way of life."

Dona Meilach (Photographer: Mel Meilach)

Not too many years ago, I would have been cleaning all the time, just in case someone might see a less than perfect home. Now, my work is the most important thing and it comes first. (Joan Schulze, exhibiting artist and teacher)

I have learned to be selfish. I have seen women who after their children have gone find that their superclean houses and organized meals and laundry are really small satisfactions. Where is the reward? However, I am not free from guilt. My efforts are spasmodic—and sometimes shamelessly neglected. (Barbara Murdock, art teacher and quilt designer, Nevada)

I think it is important to be realistic and do the best you can do and not demand more than that of yourself. I stay up all night if I am in the mood, because then I have large blocks of uninterrupted time in which to work. . . . I have been divorced for twelve years, and my children are now . . . [at about 5 different universities]. If you detect a note of smugness in my response it will be because I am juggling three jobs without losing my mind, I run my household, I run my mother's household, and I have my profession as weaver/teacher. (Momo Nagano)

I can't do all these jobs myself and do them all well. We have a wonderful Irish lady who looks after the children. I couldn't live without her—I am completely scatterbrained about children's dentist appointments, party invitations, etc. But Mary keeps track of everything. It's great being able to work with assistants and I am learning how (it's a great art). I still haven't learnt it properly but I know that's the secret of success. (Erica Wilson)

Doing all things well—that must be the pretense (and occasionally, when it works, the glory) of those of us who "work at home." It's entirely possible—nay, probable, that if one devoted all her time and energy to one or the other she might make a real go of something . . . but the circumstances of our lives really don't lend themselves to singlemindedness. (Ann La Pietra)

•

Can any woman be an artist with a full-time commitment to her work and still be an attentive mother, a passable housekeeper, a loving, supportive wife, and a contributing member of the community? Can she do all these jobs and do them all well—or are a career at home and child-rearing mutually exclusive?

Most of us are brought up to regard the ideal woman as something akin to Wonder Woman, Mighty Mom, and the Amazon. We feel we not only *can* do everything, but that we owe it to our families and ourselves. We lay on ourselves the weight of doing all things, being all things, and excelling in each or feeling guilty about our failures.

We know it's possible—every home magazine gives us a picture story of the glamorous, successful woman-executive hugging happy children goodbye as she takes off for a day of high-powered appointments, returning to entertain eight at a simple but elegant dinner she prepared while relaxing with her spouse over drinks to exchange small talk about the day. We marvel at her dazzling schedule, her brilliance and energy, her healthy children, her contented, proud, and successful husband, her trim waistline. We are sure it can be done—there's the lady who did it. Don't her kids every break their teeth falling off a bike? Doesn't the electricity ever go off at her house leaving her with wet hair and a defrosting freezer? Doesn't she ever get a headache or a bladder infection or forget her mother-in-law's birthday? Doesn't she ever hear a devastatingly critical comment from a friend, a coworker, a relative, or her husband?

Of course she does. No woman, balancing all these roles, is completely free from frustrations or conflicts or guilts over her choices. Even in the face of *proof* that we can't perform like Super Mom, we still tend to measure ourselves against that myth. Magazine articles suggest that we *can* assume several full-time jobs without visibly falling apart at the seams.

Obviously, women whose work takes them away from home need help— housekeepers, baby sitters, office help, secretaries, or assistants. And they usually have the income to make that possible. When a woman is working at home, even professionally active in her own studio, it's not as easy to justify the expenses of sitters or housekeepers. And art, as always, being long—while time is fleeting—is not necessarily going to offset the financial burden of hired help. By the time we're really making a "go" of fiber arts, our children are nearly grown and the need for a sitter is diminishing. We have to play a numbers game, shifting and scheming, taking time from one job and lavishing it on another. So if household help is not an alternative, then a new way of viewing housework may be in order.

Ruth Law, a toy maker and writer, says:

Wife and mother are a couple of words which define a woman in relation to other people and are tossed off to encompass around-the-clock versatility and diligence as resident janitor, chef, waitress, busboy, dishwasher, taxi service, etc. more personalized than money can buy.

This is a lot of work and has its own particular rewards, but it is not a life. This is mainte- nance on a grand scale. Maintenance is necessary to living, but it isn't living. In the general scheme of things in most homes, maintenance is a woman's responsibility, and the more ex- peditiously it is managed the better. When these responsibilities take up all of one's time, it is the source of discontent to many women, to their credit. They ought to be discontent.

Nowhere but in TV commercials do women discuss the relative merits of their respective methods of cleaning the toilet bowl. Brightening your wash won't brighten your day enough to pay for itself.

It is often necessary to perform numerous roles, being artist, cook, housekeeper, mother, etc. But that doesn't mean you have to excel in every area. Rose Dwight comments:

Doing things well needs to be evaluated closely. One friend of mine feels she must make home- made cookies and a big Ladies' Home Journal *dinner every night and the house must be spot- less. Another good friend, who does outstanding soft sculpture, is always complaining about her lack of time. But just last week she said, "I want to be the best headmaster's wife, the best mother, and the best soft sculptress." She is not willing to look at any of this. She doesn't know that we aren't in the Olympics and that there definitely will be no gold medalist.*

At our house we have pretty much lived in a pigsty for 15 years and if I keep cookies around for the kids I eat them myself. I have found that the children and my husband demand or want or at least seem happy with a whole lot less. . . . to tell you the truth, my family is rather happy to have me out of their hair.

Now to get back to our basic question: Can you do all these jobs and do them all really well? First, you don't personally have do them all; second, you don't *have* to do them all well. Why not be a top-notch quilter but settle for being a mediocre housekeeper, for example? Be a superb needlepointer and a great lover—but let the rewards and joys of having the shiniest floor in town fall to the lady down the block. Work at what you most enjoy. Be best at something, if that's important to you. Don't feel compelled to excel at everything, which is unlikely and unrealistic.

There are lots of ways of looking at "doing things well." My housekeeping was simplified when I let my children sleep in sleeping bags. Life is too short to hassle over unmade beds.

I next learned the great value of respecting children's rights to privacy, which means you shut their bedroom doors and don't look in.

Kids can run vacuum cleaners easily—when they are ready. If you want to keep your child's room magazine-perfect and ready to show guests, then admit that it's not the child's room, it's yours. And you jolly well *should* keep it clean yourself if it's something you want to display.

I will admit surprise when I saw seedlings sprouting from the carpeting in my daughter's room. That takes a lot of spilled water, dirt, and seeds. One friend of mine gasped over what it would do to the carpeting. Well, it obviously won't improve the carpet, but I figure that stays until she leaves for college; I can't ask it to survive longer than that.

What I am saying is that I respect her room and her way of doing (or not doing) things. She respects mine. We have a good, sound, warm, and enjoyable relationship: I think she's great and she thinks I'm great. Can I ask for more than that?

Don't nag children about inconsequential things. If they want to sleep in a dresser drawer or under a bed, why not? Co-operate with them on the goofy ideas and absurd things that intrigue them, and when you must say "no," they will accept that. If you are always denying small pleasures, all denials are suspect.

After shutting the bedroom door, the next best thing I ever did was to get household help. It is important to set that priority as early as possible. When we left student housing at Stanford and my husband took his first teaching job, I started design work. I drew the ads for postage-meter machines. Two or three drawings paid for a day's help. The best thing about household help was not being spared the work, but the change in my attitude. When I cleaned a bathroom and five minutes later found the sink covered with dirty soap drippings, I resented it. This was personal—somebody was disregarding my work or failing to value my efforts. When someone else had cleaned it, I could shrug, leave the children alone about it, and know that help would be back in a few days to clean it up again. Having household help frees me from the guilts and frustrations that sometimes result when housekeeping is neglected or postponed.

At one glorious time, help came three to four mornings a week. That meant the family breakfasted together and then all went to our respective schools or jobs. Mine was my stitching and writing at home. I have had help ever since and consider it one of the significant aids to me professionally. Although my children are grown now, I still find help, one day a week, important. It lets me relax about housekeeping, and makes me more tolerant of my husband's lax attitude about mess.

"It's so easy to spend your time driving children around, going to luncheons, coffees, showers, and meetings. If you are devoted to a craft you need to preserve that precious working time by simplifying your other life."

Jill Nordfors (Photographer: Patricia Rush)

Help is not a luxury for me—it is an essential. When necessary I can cut a lot of corners: I will cook with hamburger for a week or wear my sneakers with the toes out, but I will not give up weekly help.

Many women say help is hard to find, and I'm sure that's true. But don't overlook possibilities near home. *Tell* people what you're looking for. Call the local college, youth employment, the university or high school, and neighbors. Advertise at your local grocery or at church, and *tell* people—everyone—that you're looking. Help *is* available.

Once when I was looking for help a friend and neighbor offered to work several mornings a week. I pointed out to her that I needed someone to wash windows and clean floors. She answered that this job would allow her to be home until her youngest left for school, and to be home by noon for lunch. She could ride over on her bike, needed no car, no new clothes, and wasn't obligated to come if dental appointments or the junior-high Hallowe'en program interfered. Besides, she wanted to buy a new saw.

Another great help was a friend, a superb cook, who loved to bake bread. She had a realtor's license but preferred gourmet cooking to sales. I preferred sewing to baking bread. She agreed to bake whole-grain breads for me once a week as she was saving for a loom she had ordered. It was great to serve beautiful, nutritious home-made bread! No matter how slight your meal, this makes it hearty and elegant. And my friend saved the money for her loom. These trades are essential. Each of us should do what we enjoy and are good at, and then share by trading.

Karen Jahncke manages

by compromising, by lowering my standards of housekeeping perfection. Can you believe I actually used to scrub baseboards? I decided that when the children were grown up and I was old and gray, they would not recall me fondly to their children as that wonderful woman who kept such clean baseboards, with the neatest closets and cleanest windows in town. I hope they will remember enjoying and sharing in some of the fun things I do.

Furthermore, I am extremely fortunate in that we are able to afford a maid two days a week from 9 to 3. Since I have one young child not in school all day, this allows me two days to teach needlework at the Louisiana Crafts Council. I work on those days from 10 a.m. to 2:30 p.m and still get home in time for the children getting home from school. And I so much prefer getting out and talking to other grownups those two days to staying home and vacuuming and washing.

Judy Roderick, batik artist from Albuquerque, shares her housekeeping tasks:

I have involved the whole family in housework since it is their house too. My husband often cooks. He and my ten-year-old clean up after meals. When the house really gets bad everyone pitches in and cleans it. I do not view myself as a maid taking care of everybody. They are quite capable of doing a lot of things for themselves. This has been quite a change—which has happened gradually over the last few years. But my husband, especially, would rather have a happy wife than a spotless house.

You don't have to cook a gourmet three-course dinner every night, either. You don't even have to cook every night for that matter. Children and husbands can become good chefs.

One very effective means of avoiding doing *everything* is simply to exercise your capacity to say "no." Did it every occur to you to just say, "I'm busy and can't quit. Who would like to fix dinner?" Don't deprive your family of the joys of learning to cook—don't deny a child or husband who may have a real flair for cooking. One person does have to remain in charge, for supplies and shopping, but much of the routine cooking can be shared. Some women assign each family member to fix dinner one night a week.

Eating is partly a visual affair. A great bunch of flowers on the table, with a colorful mat in the center, along with a few sprigs of parsley and cherry tomatoes, will go a long way towards making any meal more inviting. If it's nutritious, palatable, and attractive, that's all you really need. Fortunately, some of the most nutritious foods are raw and fresh and easily prepared. It's better to have sliced apples and cheese, or some dried figs, nuts, and currants for dessert than to have a sweet baked dessert. If breakfasts are a problem (because you work late at night), bake cookies that are full of nuts, wheat germ, and oatmeal or peanut butter. Most kids will happily take milk and a handful of cookies for breakfast. It is as good a breakfast as you can give them, it leaves no pans to be washed, and it won't take half your morning.

Who cares if you take advantage of frozen or canned or dried foods? You'd be foolish not to. Take pride in your shortcuts. The woman who brags that a certain dish took her five hours to prepare may just be inefficient. Or she may assume some correlation between time and final product. Some of the worst stitcheries I've ever seen were worked on for months on end. Some of the most delightful paintings were turned out by children in about seven minutes. I don't mean to glibly disregard the relationship between craftsmanship and time, but the actual amount of time spent is not significant in the long run. The enjoyment of that time is important to the creator. The person who ultimately possesses the work probably could not care less about how many hours it took—it is the visual and aesthetic result that is enjoyed and appreciated.

I am often asked if I have someone help me with the handwork on my appliqué and my designing or quilting. The answer is "No!" When I can afford help I hire someone to wash the windows, do the floors, or the laundry. I'm not going to hire someone to do what I most enjoy, to give me time to clean the bathrooms! This question arises, I think, because we can justify hiring help for work or for jobs where there is income, but we don't feel justified hiring household help because, obviously, every semi-competent woman can manage her own home!

When I'm working on a design deadline or on a commission, I often have help on basic sewing. I have a friend who does machine sewing and assembly for me, often aiding tremendously in figuring out the mechanics and logistics of things. But the designing and hand-sewing are parts I most enjoy and could not relinquish. I'd never hire someone to do my hand-quilting (the part I like best) so that I could cook a meal. I'd rather spend the money on take-out food and do the sewing myself.

Most of us tend to make a lot of assumptions about what we have to do. Often nobody expects them of us; they are self-imposed demands. I was recently sputtering around in the laundry folding towels and wondering why I was the only one who ever did that. Then I realized that everyone else in the house would happily have stepped out of the shower and dripped all the way to the dryer to dig out a clean towel. Without every complaining. I could leave towels in the dryer or stuff a wad of them in the linen closet, or not even wash them, and no one would really notice. *I* am the one who likes clean folded towels. So I still fold them, but I don't feel put-upon. Perhaps I have been indoctrinated, as a woman, to enjoy the tidiness of an organized home. It's part of the baggage I'm still carrying around and it seems relatively a light load to me now.

Many of our housekeeping standards are like this—self-imposed. When they become really important to other members of the family, someone will eventually either do the chores, complain until you do them, or learn to ignore them. Incidentally, by appearing to enjoy household jobs yourself you make them a whole lot less odious to others. It's the white-washed fence routine in Tom Sawyer. Word games make dishes go faster, a point system for jobs can distract and reward. If these things seem distasteful to you, you probably have some other system for inviting the sharing of the routine, mechanical parts of homemaking. Nancy Papa, textile artist and writer from California, feels

Home is a shared responsibility as we all live there—though I still feel the need to be aware of chores to be done and who is available to do them. My personal housekeeping standard has gone down over the years, but it hasn't hit rock-bottom yet!

Gini Hill, fiber artist and teacher in Houston, adds:

Housekeeping is far down on my list of priorities, to the point that I'm really ashamed to have anyone come to see me. I could find time for both if I were better disciplined. I am a natural procrastinator and indulge myself by putting off what I don't like to do.

The key for me would be more efficient use of time (I waste a lot), more will power, or better yet, a full-time housekeeper. I do enjoy a clean neat house and when I do get it that way, would love to spray it with something that would make it last—I hate to do over next week what I didn't even want to do this week.

Carole Austin observes that

With many people the need to create is as strong as the need to eat and to be loved and if it is not fulfilled it is a serious thing. I try to help my students understand that it is an important and valid need and that they have the right to take care of this need without feelings of guilt. We certainly don't feel guilty eating when we are hungry.

It is easy to take on responsibilities which are not yours. My husband and I make it a policy never to commit each other's time. We can accept dinner invitations for ourselves, but not for both of us without checking first. The same rule applies to children. If an event involves a parent's time or driving, that person must be asked first.

My husband (who rarely makes assumptions about my time) was talking to a cousin on the phone one day and said to me, "When do you want them to come out—Saturday afternoon or Sunday morning?" A loaded question—I was busy and didn't want them to come at all. I answered, "You invite them whenever *you* want to have them here, and I will plan accordingly." I'll gladly entertain anyone he enjoys and wants to see, but it must be clear that they are his guests. That way, he won't decide to play tennis or run off on an errand five minutes before they are due to arrive. Their visit takes the same amount of time on my part, but my attitude is better.

When kids need their gym clothes clean by morning, it's not fair to them to let them think that the sparkling fairy comes at night and does all those little chores for them. Run the laundry, if you prefer, but let the responsibility for getting the clothes into the washer be theirs. Once you accept the responsibility, it's yours.

My son once got *D*s for an entire semester of eighth grade because he couldn't remember his gym clothes (yes, P.E. grading was based on whether or not you brought clean clothes on Monday morning!). It would have been ten times easier for me to launder his gym clothes, fold them, and have them ready to hand him as he went out the door on Monday. But *some* girl is going to be grateful to me someday! It took weeks, but he learned. I'd have done him no favor by accepting the responsibility for him.

I have seen mothers run up and down stairs five times in a morning trying to rouse a reluctant student to go to school. Why not get an alarm clock and give *him* the responsibility. When he's late, *he* has a problem with the school, not you. Nothing will cure tardiness like having to accept the responsibility! And as long as a mother will accept it, any sleepy student can figure out what to do about that.

We can take on varying kinds of responsibility. One woman in a seminar complained about her PTA involvement. Her husband was a teacher and her children were in school, so she felt obligated to help. Sometimes her help amounted to busywork, and little was accomplished. But she found it hard to actually say "no" when someone called her. We concluded that when school started in the fall, she should call the PTA chairman and *volunteer* for a job she considered worthwhile (for example, making posters and banners for the fall book fair, or taking care of the centerpiece for the Christmas open house, or driving students for a field trip). Volunteering for anything, so long as you consider it worthwhile and would enjoy it, allows you to say, "I have already volunteered my services to the PTA this year" if someone calls you up. This works for all kinds of organizations and committees.

Women artists who spend most of their waking hours at their own work often think it must be at someone else's expense. But when the time demands of multiple careers increase, it is usually a woman's own needs that are the first to be sacrificed. She often gives up her own pleasures in the continuous effort to do everything and be everything.

Because I do *many* things, I can't enjoy them all fully. I regret not having more time for friends—to develop new ones and to enjoy old ones. Carolyn Vosburg Hall adds, "I do feel sorry when I seem to be too busy for friends because people relationships are what life's all about for me. But my way of communicating with people is often through my art."

Another artist who has too much work, Carol Cheney Rome, observes that she does so many jobs she doesn't get the pleasure she should from any:

I am a conscientious person and am well organized. I am fast and thorough. Perhaps if I did not have these attributes, along with an overdose of wanting to please the world, I might take on less and enjoy it more. My greatest complaint is that I have very little time to develop my own artistry and technical expertise and feel quite behind at the moment. This is an author's occupational hazard. The next manuscript proposal comes along quicker than the jump in self-education.

Jo Reimer, fiber artist and teacher from Oregon, assesses her problem similarly:

I occasionally accept jobs which I shouldn't and then find I haven't the time or inclination to do them. I am learning to say "no"; to evaluate whether I should take on any more responsibility. There aren't enough hours in my day and I don't always use those I have well.

39

We are led to believe that women must be all-serving and self-sacrificing, which ultimately benefits no one. But we are saddled with various attitudes, some inherited and some acquired. We don't want it to look as if the family has to sacrifice cleanliness and spotless floors for our careers. (Unthinkable!) Not all of this fear is unfounded, either. Some other women will always resent your involvement in your own work. And they will delight in finding that you can't do it all, that there are some areas you've neglected—reminding you that the azalea on the porch is dying or that your child looks a little thin.

Being at home where you have to trip over the unsorted laundry and rinse a glass in order to get a drink makes it hard to ignore the demands of housekeeping, as Joyce Gross of the Mill Valley Quilt Authority observes:

Like many women who have worked at home and been accustomed to the numerous interruptions, I was guilty of allowing myself the luxury of interrupted time. When the task or job I was working on became difficult or tedious, I could always go to the kitchen or make the phone call for an appointment or do something in the garden. For example, when I was working on the Patch in Time *catalog I even found that I was scrubbing the kitchen floor instead of working on the text. That's how far I would go, saying to myself, "Well, it was terribly dirty." Let me say, Jean, that dirt doesn't move me to action more than once or twice a year, so it was an excuse.*

Now when Ed says, "What are you going to do today?" I answer, "I have to work at my desk clearing up some correspondence" or "I have to prepare for my class." I'm not sure it makes any difference to him, but it takes it out of the realm of a hobby for me.

Any woman will exhaust herself racing in the tracks of Mighty Mom. Settle for doing your best rather than collapsing in the pursuit of perfection. Don't fret over household tasks undone and work unfinished. Keep your sense of humor. Remember that anyone in your family will enjoy a hug and five whole minutes devoted entirely to him more than he'll enjoy a polished floor.

Peggy Ritsi has a clear idea of what is essential to her:

If I were not allowed . . . to be myself, I'd be a terribly unhappy woman, having a clean and honorably domestic house. My house is a home because I come first. If I could not be happy with myself, how could I project happiness in my home and to those I surround? I love my husband, children, and household activities, but they would never think of standing in the way of me as an individual.

At one time I was a slave to my house—no longer! I am a slave to me (and my husband thinks a slave to him even though there are no buttons on his shirt, and his p.j.s are falling off because there is no time to repair—only embellish). I perform as a complete woman, am a better mother, certainly a better wife, and the house is clean. I love to cook, and it has never stood in the way of my creativity, but enhanced it.

Anne Syer, batik artist from California, says:

It's easier to have crafts as your work than other types of jobs. There's not such a big gulf between work and home. I used to have some "straight" . . . jobs in education and I always felt there was one "professional" me and one "real" me. I feel good that my family can know what my work is and see me doing it. I remember wondering what mysterious things my dad did when he went to New York City "to the office."

Elsbeth Ramos, fiber artist from Monterey, develops these thoughts further:

I find time because art is such an integral part of my life. The line between art and life in my daily activities is not clearly defined.

It has not been easy, but now that two of my three children are teenagers they begin to see me as a human being. It has been difficult for them to see me in the role of a serious artist-craftswoman until recently. Now that I am exhibiting, selling as well as teaching, they are gaining a respect (although my oldest son admits he does not understand my work) for what I do.

And Dona Meilach, artist, teacher and author of many craft books, adds her thoughts:

I don't do all jobs well. I give some jobs priority . . . and relegate the others in various orders of importance. For instance, I'm not a creative or fancy cook. Meals are adequate, nutritious, but my recipe repertoire is limited (my daughter's comment). I spend a minimum of time on meal-making. Food shopping is done once a week and anything I don't have by the end of the week . . . I make do with something else. Shopping for myself has become a luxury which is often frustrating when I need something to wear.

Dee Mosteller, quilter and writer for television and magazines, has this advice for women who have studios or work space at home:

My best advice to persons who would work at home: (1) find a very private spot to work in, and never let anyone come in unannounced; (2) keep your working spot out of sight of the living area and vice versa; (3) have an answering service so you can ignore the telephone when your work is going well . . . and still be comfortable in the knowledge that you can find out later who called; (4) don't let yourself go even one day without doing some work on at least one major project, even if you have severe writer's block or a hurt painting hand; (5) try to live with someone who has a steady job and income—that's beneficial in two ways—it gets him/her out of your hair all day or night, and you don't have that terrible pressure of financial problems which can kill all creative drive.

Carole Austin does

some jobs well and some not so well depending on their importance to me. I despise housecleaning but cannot stand a dirty house. So I set aside every Thursday to clean it and I work fast. I do what has to be done to remain civilized according to my own definition. My one and only self-indulgence is that I have a cleaning woman twice a month. I give up other things for this because it is the most important to me. I no longer do fancy cooking except when entertaining and as a treat for my family on Sunday. . . .
I do not neglect my family though sometimes it is at a cost to myself. Summer taxi service is the thing that really tears me up because I can't find time for myself. . . . time spent in a car is such wasted time. . . . But on the other hand I want my children to lead active, productive lives of their own and in most cases they cannot do it without my driving.

B. J. Adams, fiber artist from Washington, D.C., says she no longer does as much entertaining as she used to, or "as much housework as I used to think necessary, and only when company or entertaining gets in the way of deadlines do we have any timing problems."

Hard as it is to admit (for all of us who aspire, in spite of ourselves, to be Amazons), something has to give. When there is too much to do, women tend to give up their own work and small pleasures. I have been pleased in the past few years to have more commissions and more invitations to lecture and to teach. But sometimes I envy my students who still have time to make quilts for their friends. I recently realized I was the only one in the class I was teaching with no time to sew. So I went home and started two quilts as gifts for friends. Neither was finished by Christmas, but then both were underway.

Madge Copeland, textile artist and teacher in California, made this observation about time and work:

I am a good artist all the time, a good teacher most of the time, not too terrific a mother and wife. We eat a pan of spaghetti until it's gone—three dinners in a row. I do not read to the children. The kid's clothes are always repaired and they leave home with teeth brushed.

But if I'm frustrated then I'm mean. I figure it's better if I'm happy and they have to struggle with academics on their own. I'm in the minority in this—there is an abundance of overachieving Moms for kids in this community . . .

Occasionally, when teaching or lecturing, I suddenly notice how great everyone looks. My own hair may be three weeks overdue for a cutting, and I'm wearing a winter dress on a summer day because I can't bear to take time to shop, and I hate to sew clothes. I choose to do my work first. The fun of clothes, hair and vanity gets left adrift to be rescued another day. (It'll soon be autumn and my too-warm clothes will once more be appropriate.)

I find it difficult to say "no" because many of the opportunities are so inviting. There are lots of things one can *readily* say "no" to. But if I'm invited to teach in Hawaii and Calgary and New York, they *all* sound great. I want to do it all. So it's back to priorities. Sometimes I simply have to stop travel to restore that precarious but more satisfying balance with my own creative work. I cannot (alas) do it all.

I share a common concern about a "spreading beam" since I sit so much. I go on periodic diets, until I have a deadline. Then I feel pressured and somehow have the feeling that if I get my mouth in motion my brain will automatically get into gear. My sometimes co-author Joyce Aiken once estimated that we gained five pounds with every manuscript that became due. Part of our Superwoman role is the assumption that we must also have a recognizable facsimile of the Superwoman body.

Some days I wish I could just sort through my clothes, or organize my mess of recipe cards. And those tasks take on the aura of a luxury. It's when I'm working with a group of students or finish a quilt for one of my children or see a coverlet I designed on a magazine cover that the satisfactions are fantastic. But there are always choices, constant decisions. There is never enough time, as batik artist Tricia Klem notes:

It is possible to be fiber artist and homemaker, just like with any other regular job. But even doing my work at home I find there are sacrifices to make—mainly not being free to do other things, to take a walk or start a painting. There is not enough time. The more I do, the more I want to do. And sometimes I wish I were spending more time doing things with my family or just doing nothing by myself.

Barbara Brabec, magazine publisher, describes her own pace:

I am a "workaholic" and would willingly go from daybreak to late evening every day of the year but for my husband who reins me in and makes me take "days off" each week to putter. But I always putter with a guilty conscience, thinking about the work piling up in the office.

Some of the solutions mentioned in this chapter will be appropriate for you and others will not. But when you're receptive, when you need help, a single comment can sometimes strike home and change your outlook.

I try to keep in mind that anything worth doing is worth doing poorly. That isn't snide. There are so many people who say, "I really wish I could do this or that but I don't do it well." Then they do nothing. (Ann deWitt)

I accomplish a great deal because I consciously decide how to use my time. I decide what I have to do, what I want to do and then work around the two. I'm not always consistent: I find that I am very irritable if I spend too many days just on routine junk. Too many women allow themselves to be used (maybe even enjoy allowing themselves to be used) and then find justification in being the martyr. There is a lot of bitterness that grows in this situation; self-punishment as well as punishment of others for the sterile life one may find oneself in. (Jody House)

I usually feel that I have three jobs: (1) Weaver, (2) Wife/mother/housekeeper, (3) Teacher. Since we work at home, many people don't consider that we really work and therefore should be available for committees, phone calls, bake sales, etc.

We do have an advantage in working at home, being "our own bosses," in that we can quickly put a roast on for supper or put a cake in the oven, throw some laundry in, run down to school for a class play, etc. We have a freedom and flexibility that can be very tempting without some discipline. (Sharon Lappin Lumsden, who describes herself as a weaver, wife/mother, teacher, all-round good person, from Illinois)

My day starts early–I wake at 5:30, my mind is working and thinking. I get up and do. If my work is in the thinking stages, I will do quiet household chores while thinking. If my work is in the working stages, I work until breakfast time, take care of breakfast, then back to work (or play). I use every minute all day long. (Ginger Carter, designer and teacher from Missouri)

In order to save time and money, I rarely wear makeup. I have my hair cut short so that I can wash it in the shower, and I wear wash-and-wear items. I never iron. I spend as little time as possible in the kitchen. We eat high-protein meals, no TV dinners nor Jack-in-the-Box take-homes, and I don't bake, not even Xmas cookie dough ornaments. The dishes from all seven of us (remember the four cats) are dumped into the dishwasher where they rattle away. (Packing them in methodically is beyond my patience.) I spent 15 married years without a dishwasher. What an idiot I was!!! (Nancy Lipe)

Sometimes this great enthusiasm for doing many different things and excelling at them has another side to it which takes shape in a feeling of futility because I know deep down that I have limits and I will in fact not be able to do everything. (Lynda Lanker)

I had to learn about priorites the hard way, through years of trying to please everyone else (just try that when you're a minister's wife and see what happens–everyone else knows just what you're supposed to be like!), and of never being able to say "no," and consequently of suffering migraine headaches sometimes for weeks on end. Now I can set two types of priorities–one of values and activities in my life over the long range, and the other of priorities for the day. Creativity has a high priority in my life, but if we're having dinner guests at night I can't spend the whole day stitching. I must temporarily postpone acting on a high priority (or get super-creative with a gorgeous dessert) because today includes an activity whose importance supersedes stitching. The reason I feel two sets of priorities are important is that if I lose sight of the long-range ones I find it very easy to let my day's priorities get mixed up, and pretty soon a week will go by without my lifting a needle because so many other "important" things came up, and I kept postponing needlework. I need to keep constantly aware of priorities–not a long, rigid set, but the most important for my good and my family's. (Ricky Clark)

4.
The Playpen in the Studio

"While my children were growing up I enjoyed them and centered my activities around them. I did 'my thing' in small doses. I do believe that I was a better wife and mother because I always had several stitchery projects going."

Jacqueline Enthoven (Photographer: Douglas Jones)

The event that got my energies channeled creatively was the birth of my son five years ago. Before that, when I had all the time in the world, I had thoughts of writing children's books. From time to time I would try it; my idea of writing was to turn on my typewriter and drink wine until I fell off my stool. Basically I had such a low self-image that I thought that every other bright young thing with time on her hands was wanting and needing to write or make art of some kind and was likely to do better than I, so why try? I was very depressed. (Beth Gutcheon)

It was when the children were small that I felt the strongest need to express myself artistically, somehow. (Peggy Moulton)

It wasn't until I quit working and Elizabeth was born that I actually picked up the needle in a creative way and began to meld the dormant interest in textiles with my ability to draw. (Wilanna Bristo, designer from Texas)

We had that all settled before we were married. I knew what I needed to feel whole and with what intensity I would pursue it. But I did want children and can honestly say that I've never neglected them. Rather, we felt we grew with them. Everything one learns in life is applicable in some way in every other field. As a parent I learned how a mind grows, flows, how to teach—how to learn. Endless things. (Joan Michaels-Paque)

My friend, Mrs. J., graduated from Stanford, and won a Phi Beta Kappa key which she let her children use as a teething ring. (Ann deWitt)

I came before the children and they just fit into the scheme . . . with patience they learned not to touch and it just worked into a way of life. (Marilyn Judson, calligrapher, stitcher and author from California)

●

Any mother who removes the last half of a dripping peanut butter and jelly sandwich from her new quilt top probably considers putting the sandwich-eater up for adoption. Applesauce does not improve the warp threads on a loom and the slush of a snow cone won't visibly enhance a drawing. A play pen in the studio has its low points and frustrations, as well as some heartwarming benefits.

Mothering is a full-time, 24-hour-a-day job, and women extract varying degrees of satisfaction from it. What is satisfying for one is not necessarily fulfilling for another. There is no one right answer, though we are often led to believe there is.

Articles about us see-saw, convincing us on one hand that only an uncaring woman would leave a baby in someone else's hands, and on the other that women must play an increasingly important role in all facets of society. Just when we're convinced that the quality, not the quantity of time is more important, we are numbed by the headline asserting that a mother's duty, always, is to "be there."

45

Capable, caring mothers *do* pursue their own careers and they, too, have happy, well-adjusted, and much-loved children.

Fiber artists often ride their bicycles down the tight rope between these two extremes. Precarious and wobbly as the ride may be, we find we *can* be with our children and pursue our work. But not easily. The home studio resolves some of the conflict which society imposes about being a good mother as well as a productive citizen. It adds the difficulty of rocking the cradle while plying the needle.

There are many valid approaches to mothering which meet the child's needs without ignoring the mother's. It is a matter of finding the one which suits the temperament, interests and priorities of those involved. Every mother develops her own way of handling her responsibility. She has to consider the individual needs of her child and herself, her experience, her professional commitment, finances, and personal preferences. The methods and means of child-rearing vary greatly. Some mothers are cautious, careful, and completely in control, giving deliberate attention to each decision. Others are relaxed and casual, letting things move at their own pace. Where one mother will cuddle a lot, another will yell, and most of us rely on a combination of hugs, threats, love, talk, demands, reason, and large measures of hope and faith, clinging desperately and hopefully to the theory that heredity, is, after all, far more important than environment.

Motherhood enriches one's life but it should not become one's life. It can be a marvelous addition because it plunges us chin-deep in the stream of humanity. But if children's interests supplant the mother's interests entirely, they become a limitation. If children are to grow, parents must grow.

Most mothers find that the greatest difficulty in combining family with fibers comes during years when children are preschool age. It is then that demands on the mother's time seem relentless; it is during those years that she often feels it has been months since she has been to the bathroom by herself, or had a shower in privacy. It probably has.

The problems of single mothers are more complex. Having the full responsibility of children gives these women almost no time for their work unless they have outside help or assistance of some kind. They can at least identify the difficulty and openly search for alternatives and assistance. Some women, even though living with husbands, are essentially single parents, but the situation isn't defined as such so it's even more difficult to cope with. There is no way to describe the importance of a good father-child relationship, and the value of shared responsibility. I know that I could never have accomplished my own work without a husband who took his role of parenting seriously.

When my son was two, my husband completed his term as a Navy pilot and we both decided to go to graduate school. With the help of a fine day nursery and a very supportive partner, I was able to complete my M.A. at Stanford University. It was exciting, hard work, and we all thrived on it.

A neighbor informed me on various occasions that I was ruining my son's psyche by "forcing him" into nursery school. She knew (by the way her own son screamed whenever she left him) how bad it was for the unformed child. My child was independent, and sometimes even indifferent to the fact that I was leaving him. I took this as a sign that he felt confident in the knowledge that I was not abandoning him.

However, I was not immune to doubts and guilts thus planted by supposedly well-meaning friends. Antagonism on the part of other young mothers occasionally emerged because I was not staying put in the proper wife-mother role. There was, however, much positive support from faculty women and other women in graduate school who also had small children. That kind of support was crucial to me.

Only once did I really feel anguish over leaving my son. On the last day of my last semester he decided he did not want to go to nursery school. I had two final exams that day, and I think he sensed my anxiety. It was the one day out of the year that I could not skip classes and stay home with him. He cried (only briefly, the teacher informed me later) but I suffered over that morning for weeks. I know now that 20 minutes of unhappiness does not overwhelm everything else in a child's life. He was home with me all day every day after that. But I do know the overwhelming feelings of guilt and the exhausting strain of being pulled in two directions at once.

The following year my husband went on to further graduate work and I elected to stay at home and pursue my art. In the next two years I plunged headlong into my stitchery (then almost unheard of), gave birth to my daughter, had my first one-woman show, and wrote my first magazine article. I found that being at home offered a marvelous opportunity to pursue my own work.

Many, many women have worked their art and home lives together in this same enriching way. I felt fortunate that I *could* stay home. My children were never neglected (nor were they entertained) by me. The women who have it hard, in my view, are those who find it financially necessary to go out of their own homes to work. I personally find that home and family offer their own particular pleasures and marvelous rewards, without being *totally* satisfying. My work offers satisfactions and pleasures, but it cannot be my whole life. I want and need both. I'd be unwilling to give up either.

For me, child-rearing was an exciting, challenging, and rewarding job. It was not confining—children expanded my horizons without limiting them. I took them places, but not everywhere, as both were terribly active and curious and appallingly uncautious. I've enjoyed their company, and find many children to be more responsive and interesting (and interested) than many adults. Listening to a child learn to speak, think, explore, and learn was fascinating. I would never willingly relinquish those pleasures to anyone else. That doesn't mean it wasn't often hard work and sometimes frustrating and unnerving.

Child-rearing is not easy. (Neither is quilting or lecturing or designing.) I had the help of one or two college-age babysitters, which gave me some uninterrupted time for myself and my work. My idea of the way to use a sitter was to have him or her take the kids to the zoo or out for hamburgers or to the library, leaving me in the peace and quiet of home. Sometimes a sitter stayed with one child so I could take the other with me: one child is easy. Sitters were synonymous with fun and doing exciting things and going places, so my children enjoyed them and didn't feel they were "stuck with the sitter" while their parents got to go somewhere special. The separations were crucial to my sanity and to my enjoyment of the children when they were at home.

In student housing we had a babysitting pool. Later I traded sitting with my neighbor whose backyard was adjacent. That way either of us could be free to run an errand or shop—and of course it takes a tenth as long to do that alone as it does with several small children. Since kids do enjoy these excursions (even the grocery store seems an adventure) I would often take one. Never both, if I could possibly arrange otherwise! With two children, the total is infinitely greater than the sum of the parts.

Not everyone responds in the same way to the presence of babies or children and their constant need for care. To some, motherhood is confining, unnerving, and depressing. For me it was the excuse I'd always wanted to stay home and do my own work.

Many women find little satisfaction in the company of youngsters. The conversations seem pointless and they feel reduced to baby talk. It has been my experience that children ask profound questions, make no assumptions, take nothing for granted, question your most fundamental beliefs. It is exciting. But the woman who loves her work and prefers to be away from home loves her children no less. It is often a matter of personalities, children's ages, financial need, career opportunities, and the period at which one has arrived in her own work, or a combination of these. Obviously we must all sort through our priorities and needs and find the best individual solution. And then accept the fact that other women will have other solutions that will be equally valid for them. I am disappointed to hear one woman criticizing another for finding a solution which varies radically from her own. If it works, use it. If it works well, use it and rejoice.

Weaver and fiber artist Rivkah Sweedler found it very difficult

being a mother, being home and doing dirty diapers and dishes all the time with my college degree tucked away somewhere and four years of having worked and earned a salary to support the family, and suddenly just being nothing but Dr. ——'s wife. I think I'm at a better place now . . . since I've been weaving, getting really involved in it, I've been feeling so much better about myself, as a person—beginning to feel some validity in myself . . . a value the family recognizes, the kids don't resent my weaving. But then we do have the problem that there's no one around to cook dinner, do the laundry.

It's one thing we're really trying to work out—find some way in which we can spread that work out, share the roles—perhaps among more than just two adults. We're looking for solutions or alternatives.

Certainly, if you find that children interfere with your work, you should find a compromise. You need time for yourself, time to maintain your mental balance. If family finances allow, hire a sitter. If you think you can't afford one, re-examine your list of luxuries and essentials—maybe sitters go on the essential list and re-seeding the lawn becomes a luxury. Many co-op nurseries, shared homes, and communes have developed to help meet these needs.

If squeezing money out of the budget is impossible, look to other sources. Channel any money earned from your craft into babysitting. Or set up a neighborhood sitters' pool. You take five or six kids one morning a week, and do something special. Build a box city in the backyard or make clay-dough animals. Devote your time to them in the limited hours they are all yours. In exchange, other mothers take their turns and you have four free mornings a week. Everybody gains.

Find the help you need. Hire sitters when you can; trade with neighbors when you can't. When a friend or relative says, "Let me know when I can do anything to help," *let them know*. Explain your need for a morning to yourself—maybe it can become a weekly event. Husbands can enjoy excursions with the children, so if they don't make plans and arrangements themselves, help them set up a weekly outing of some kind.

I used to dream of having 24 hours a day for my own work. Then, one day when my children were small, my husband took them on a trip, leaving me with a Utopian five days. I suddenly found that I needed the interruptions—I wasn't capable of working nonstop. I'd get up and move around, feeling at loose ends. Perhaps I could have gotten used to it, but the breaks seemed to be an important aspect of the timing.

Now that my children are grown, I find I provide interruptions in my work. I pour a lot more coffee than I drink, but walking out to the kitchen relaxes the shoulder muscles and gives me a chance to refocus my eyes. The change of pace is relaxing and these spaces become pauses rather than interruptions.

Perhaps the reason many of us accomplish so much while our children are small is that we are forced to make the most efficient use of every scrap of available time. I have never been a slave to my children but have always had my work, so they've accepted it and enjoyed it. As small children they entertained themselves, just as I did—thoroughly absorbed in what they were doing. Parental attitudes are often reflected in children's behavior—if you are involved in work you enjoy, they sense that; if you are not at ease, if you're frustrated and unsettled about your life, they sense that, too, and react, making it even more difficult.

The solution to the dilemma of having both time for one's children and time for one's work is not just organization, as Cam Smith Solari says:

I first thought that if I was just organized enough I could take care of a baby and everything else I had going too. What I hadn't counted on is that, unlike all of my other projects and errands, the baby was very unpredictable.

As he got older I noticed his needs changed but he always had needs and always needed my time. I soon discovered that the only time I really had for my work, which included photography, promoting, and the house, clothes and meals, was when he was sleeping. And some days he would only sleep an hour or so.

I really have strong feelings that an infant needs to explore, to have someone there. It should be a time when he gets whatever he needs. I was getting pretty good at having the baby play where I was working and arranging to do my work in bits, around his needs and adventures, but it was beginning to look like I couldn't be both the mother who was there all the time and keep my own work going at the rate I had been doing it. My solution was to hire someone to play with Brian, which would free me to do enough work to be able to afford to pay for the help. This has really turned out well.

I got someone who takes him on walks, plays with him and talks to him, changes his diaper and follows after him to catch him when he is about to fall on his head or get into the garbage. She also does housework and makes lunch and works a regular business week from 8 a.m. to 5 p.m. . . . The nice part about this arrangement is that I am working at home so I really don't have to leave my baby. I'm breastfeeding him, and I also take lots of breaks just to play with him, and he crawls around where I can see him, so I really am there for him, while at the same time with someone else there to be responsible for handling his needs, I don't have to be interrupted.

This system only works if I use the time to produce and actually bring in some income, so

I find that even with the extra help I have to be more organized than ever before. I guess one of the scary things I had to confront was knowing I was going to have to really make my work go right to be able to afford it. But it is working out well. I'm happy getting to do my work and I also feel good about having the baby taken care of in a way that is great for him and lets me be with him.

Some artists recognize the tremendous involvement in time and energy which children require and avoid the conflict by determining not to have children. Helen Bitar has not had children

because I know that they take a lot of time—and that would be taken away from my work. I think a lot of serious artists do not have children because their work becomes their children.

Florence Pettit decided early:

I sorted my priorities when I was about seven: I was going to be an artist. My values were easy to set: both my mother and father thought everything I did was wonderful, and they gave me a good mind and an excellent art education. When I was about 20 I decided not to marry because it would interfere with my career. But at 27 I fell in love (hadn't counted on that) and wanted to get married. However, the pattern continued the same: he thought everything I did was wonderful, too, and encouraged and abetted every idea I ever had. He still does.

Beth Gutcheon says:

I don't see how I could have more than one child. I wouldn't care to have less, either, but there was a stage when the difficulty of dealing with an active toddler and my own professional obligations was almost more than I could bear.

I enjoyed having two children, but did not choose to have more. Some days it seemed that two took *all* the time there was. I might as well have had five—they couldn't take *more* time than that!

Bonnie Bartell says:

When our child was young I didn't even try to do much in the creative line except to invent stories, games, swings, and toys. He is now grown and gone from home and has matured rather well, I think, and is worth every minute I invested in him.

Fiber artists with home studios do have an advantage. They can be available to give small children the support and nurturing they need—and still be productive. Further, a lot of criticism and condemnation can be avoided. Obviously, if your work is important to you, you will do it. But many working women still find it very difficult to confront the negative attitudes of family and society toward their work. In spite of tremendous gains made through the women's movement, many women encounter biases against their work outside the home—they are "damned if they do and damned if they don't." So studios at home avoid this aspect of opposition, releasing the energy sometimes spent in feeling either defensive or guilty to be channeled into more creative uses.

If you are successful (in your home studio), you can count on being criticized for the neglect of your children (not by your own children, incidentally). If you have just published a book, written in a kitchen that would traumatize Mr. Clean, you may also encounter criticism. Someone doing just one job adequately will assail you for not doing two jobs perfectly.

Much juggling and shifting is required to maintain a household with small children. Jody House says, regarding this:

With me it is the constant interruptions from children that are hard to take. You have to be strong and explain that this time is yours but at the same time tell them when you can do what they want done and then do it. There are some things you cannot do, and they should learn this. Be direct and honest, don't make excuses. We must learn that constant self-sacrifice is a terrible thing for all involved. It leads to bitterness and hate.

Regarding interruptions, Margot Carter Blair, designer, author, and a mother of six, adds:

I have learned to say "No" without feeling guilty when the children try to interrupt me in my work. If I am forced to work while they are home, possibly on a deadline, they have a tendency to be rude. I tell them it is impolite to interrupt one who is reading or talking, and my work is no different. I ask them to please approach me by saying, "Excuse me, Mom, I would like to talk to you when you have a minute" (or something similar). This way, when I can take a break, I do then resolve the problem at hand. It is important to follow up so they will not feel left out.

For me, noise has always been a big factor. I like quiet—no radio, no stereo, no television. Children seem to love sounds of all kinds, simultaneously. Separate areas for small children help (bedrooms, play houses, tree houses, forts, etc.). We moved to the country when the children were small and the open space made a tremendous difference. Indoors, they had record players in their rooms. I didn't forbid their playing records in the kitchen/living room/studio area—but I'd wait until we were baking or cleaning and then suggest they choose a record for all of us. That way I could express an interest, share their enthusiasms, and they could then accept that I didn't want their "music" when I was writing.

Bev Rush, stitcher, author, editor, and photographer, says

The overlap is noise more than space. I like a quiet house best, and I'm surrounded by people who like radios, TV, or stereos going—it seems like full blast. There's not too much overlap on hours and compromises on loudness are possible, but I do find myself occasionally wishing for a studio on a beach with no one nearby.

Few things fascinate children more than "making things." When I worked on quilts, appliquéing blocks depicting bears, grandma's wheelbarrow, the tree house, or the jar full of caterpillars and bugs, my children were enchanted. They have dragged every child in the neighborhood in to "see what my mother is making." They have never brought home a single friend for the purpose of showing how well I had cleaned the house. And of course, we think we're doing it for them!

It's a rare toddler who doesn't want to sit on the kitchen counter and watch the magic of cookie-making or bread-kneading. Similarly, few children remain uninterested in a mother's handwork or in making things. The joy in watching is almost overwhelming if the work is being done *for* the child. A favorite ladybug sewn to a shirt pocket can color the whole world for a five-year-old. Wall hangings that illustrate favorite stories or a family camping trip or a child's new bike lets the child share in some of the pleasure you find in creating. It helps him understand your need to do things for your own pleasure.

What kinds of things will your children remember? Stop, and re-evaluate. Will they recall being punished for tearing a new jacket, or will they remember the rabbit you sewed over the tear? Was there a kitten you embroidered on a pocket to ease the parting when a pet cat was run over? Or a verse you wrote (ostensibly from the "tooth fairy") when the two front teeth fell out? We can all choose what kinds of things we'd like our children to recall.

Many women have found their children to be an unending source of ideas. Margot Carter Blair points out:

When children are young they are the source of an incredible amount of inspiration. Their clear, uninhibited, and uncluttered approach to an idea can help give the most beautiful results with shades of folk-art honesty. Their art is refreshing to me and it has been a great source. I have transferred many of the ideas, the shapes, and the colors, forms, etc. to my work. The incredible proportions their work assumes . . . . I love it.

Joan Michaels-Paque expresses similar feelings:

I personally need contact with children. They are my touchstone. Now that our own children are grown we have two "surrogate sons," three and five. They are children of close friends and we consider them part of our family.

The first five years of a child's life are most important and I think it is a birthright to have parents who feel that way. When asked by young, impatient, talented mothers how to succeed in the arts I tell them honestly that "under fives" should be at the top of their priority lists. That's the time to lay groundwork for the future.

The pleasure of having children around most of the time has been expressed over and over by fiber artists who have experienced it. Karen Jahncke says:

To me the nicest thing about the work that I do is that I can do it at home. There is no way that I would want to isolate myself completely from the children—if I did, I guess I would have to work in a studio. I don't think they resent time you spend on your work when they understand what it is you are doing and can share it.

Author and stitcher Carolyn Vosburg Hall adds:

Long ago I had some hard days hassling little kids through long hot days and wondering what good my MFA was doing me, but now I have just written and illustrated two children's books, I Love Popcorn and I Love Ice Cream, I realize that having kids was vital to doing children's books. So instead of bemoaning the fact that I might have been a greater artist if I hadn't had to spend so much time with the family, I say to myself . . . if I hadn't had the kids, I might not have been able to write those books.

Many young mothers have expressed a concern to me about keeping children out of their work. My own approach has always been to involve them—give them some of whatever you are working with. Naturally, you don't give a ten-month-old baby a box of pins, and you must be cautious about scissors and needles. But small children can handle blunt-ended scissors, and when they have their own they are much more apt to leave yours alone.

One mother bought her children a Salvation Army typewriter so that her own would be "off limits."

Another mother, Diane Bower, comments:

I never try to keep my children "out of my work." They share my reverence for sheep, equipment, and organized messes. In fact, I frequently mobilize the neighborhood children when I need 3,000 dandelion blossoms picked or huckleberries harvested for just the right dyebath. Their kookie mother is simply one facet of their environment.

"I don't even try to keep my children out of my work," says Jackie Vermeer.

When I'm writing, it is frustrating; then the only answer is to take a break. A little attention now, and children will be much more willing to leave you alone later. When I'm making something, they just share the materials. Of course, their work is important for my children's crafts books, so I really need their help. But even when I'm doing something else I find it is best to share—and try to be patient. Eventually they'll go to bed. . . .

Ann deWitt writes, "When my kids were small I made one rule: *do not use my sewing machine or else.* But I bought them one to play with. It's a dear old Wilcox and Gibbs chain-stitch machine and they loved it."

According to Elizabeth Fuller, California designer and teacher, her daughters "just naturally loved felt-tip pens, oil crayons, sewing scraps, and puppet theaters, so we worked together. Their drawings often inspired the dolls and first wall hangings I made. After a time they grew up to other interests—I didn't."

And Karen Jahncke

gave up the search for perfection. During my day I feel the children come first. So this means sometimes when everyone goes bananas, I just put down my work and we go to the park to let off steam. I do a lot of work at night after they are in bed because of this.

Providing children their own materials certainly helps. But there are some kinds of work and some times when we cannot tolerate graham-cracker crumbs or honey on everything. Then keeping children out is a matter of their respecting your work (if they are old enough) or of having it out-of-bounds or out-of-reach (if they are younger).

Ilene Ferrini-Tuttle says it's simple to keep children out of one's work:

Threaten them with death if they touch your stuff. Sometimes I worked with the children around when I gave them art projects they could handle while I worked, and sometimes I devised special art projects I did with them (macramé, collage, etc., etc.) and they now say they liked that experience, although none of them have become artists. Generally, though, my work and materials were out of bounds for them; we provided them with their own paint boxes, paper, etc. They also took art classes for children, and that helped them to relate better to what I was doing, I think.

Another designer says, "As a last resort, I yell at them!" And another artist states that she

had to be rather tyrannical in claiming territory for my work: in making it clear that my scissors are important tools and not to be violated by others. I keep the door closed to my studio and ask the family to stay out when I am not in. I tell them I have a $1,000 quilt in process and they will be responsible for it if the dog pees on it due to their negligence!

I do enjoy having my daughters in and out of the studio when I am working. When they were smaller, we all used to work on projects together. Kids develop capabilities just by being ex-

posed to materials; this is one of the ways their lives have been enlarged by my work. I find that they often have good solutions to some of my design problems! I enjoy the interchange.

A fabric designer added:

When I need quiet (which I do when I am designing), I try to work when everyone is out of the house. During the school year this is easy. In the summer I have given up doing serious designing; it's too frustrating trying to control a situation that involves others' lives.

Certainly if you have a baby, the needs of the baby must come first. You no longer have a choice about that—you have already made the decision! But they do grow up in a few years. I found the ages from one and a half to two and a half to be the most trying. They are the years when strong-willed and agile toddlers can climb anywhere without understanding any of the reasons or explanations given not to. Apparently oblivious to danger, they require more constant attention during this year. These are also the years of creative discovery and word forming. After two and a half communication improves. From then on, children seem to be a greater joy and pleasure each year.

But to enjoy your children, to allow them to become real people, you must be a real person. You must not have the feeling that you have sacrificed, denied yourself, or failed to realize some potential of your own. If these feelings lurk, you must first decide what it is you want to do, and then figure out a way to do it.

Ricky Clark offers this advice:

Keeping one's eye on long-range priorities is important to avoid the helpless, bogged-down feeling we all get when our children are infants. They do grow up, and even when they're little there are ways to find time for yourself.

First, you can (if you can afford it) hire a babysitter for two hours even once a week, and spend those two hours on yourself, either at home or away with a friend or in a class. If you can't afford it, you can trade kids with a friend so each of you gets a specified time to herself regularly. Or you can join a babysitting co-op in which mothers do the sitting for points with which they "pay" other mothers. Or you can take classes at the Y or churches which hire sitters for a very nominal fee to the mothers participating. You can also spend your children's nap times on your projects instead of housework.

One way I get a lot done is to treat my days like office work days. I do household jobs until 9 a.m. Then I quilt until noon, stop to serve lunch to whoever is around—also to get some exercise and change myself—quilt from 1 to 5 p.m. and then do family things the rest of the day. If I'm really pressured I don't even answer the phone but tell the boys to call their father if they need to and let Dave know I'm home but not taking calls.

After children are in school, life alters considerably. It is then a matter of making the best possible use of those glorious free or open hours. Eleanor A. Van de Water, artist and teacher from Washington, always uses her prime morning hours for her stitching. Then when the children get home from school, they all make the beds and do the dishes together. When children have problems, it is so much easier to talk about them while they are doing things. She would

love to have studio space. But there has been an advantage in not having a studio. The whole family is really understanding. . . . I've worked in close proximity with the children, have a very close rapport with them. We're awfully good friends, my teenage children and I. We enjoy one another. They respect my work in a way that I doubt would have happened if I'd been isolated or away from them.

54

Much housework is simply routine and offers a good time to talk with children. They help, following you from washer to drier or sink to cupboard. And they generally learn to share the work, particularly if your attitude about it is positive. (Which, if you've had six uninterrupted hours in your studio that day, it probably will be.) Most children love helping and the activity itself makes for good conversation time. They enjoy doing the things you enjoy. If you expect them to do just the jobs they think are "yukky," of course they are going to notice.

One artist-mother finds that "much of the mundane housework time is also the time I talk and listen to the children's problems or pleasures. We both work together as we talk. These are very precious moments."

Access is often what children need—and the phone is a marvelous boon. Marilyn Heise says her children always have access. They can "interrupt me whenever they wish, at home or at work. I listen, determine which is more important at the moment, work or the needs of that child, and I decide, not always pleasing everyone."

There are as many ways of getting children to participate in running the household as there are households—point systems, games, pay for work, bargains, threats, rewards, cooperation and sharing. Each family seems to work out which one is successful, or at least satisfactory. But it is certainly unfair to a child to let him grow up assuming that all houses come equipped with a full-time maid (mother) who automatically anticipates and responds to all needs. I feel strongly that children ought to have the opportunity to learn to cook and to clean up. It takes a little patience at first, but it is well worth the investment of time in the long run.

Joyce Aiken, teacher and designer, mentioned previously, as sometimes co-author, says of her sons:

The kids found out long ago that clean socks came out of a washing machine which they had filled and turned on rather than out of a sock drawer in their room. They have always helped me with my work. They have sanded, painted, sawed, hooked yarns, and done any other job they were interested in. Sometimes for love . . . mostly for $1 an hour.

Margot Carter Blair points out:

With eight people in our home, everyone does something to contribute to the mess; therefore, everyone helps with the chores. It works. The kids are excited about mom's activities and projects. They know their work is very important as it supports the whole. They are properly praised and reprimanded, loved and loved. We now see the results. . . . great training for the kids and it has liberated mom! I do not live under squelched resentments of being stuck with all the work and believe this is really the secret. We all share exciting things and discoveries, work well done, etc., and this breeds a great deal of good feelings about ourselves.

Madge Copeland says her children "love what I do but they don't insist on getting involved. I love what they do and I don't get involved either."

Joan Michaels-Paque adds:

Textiles are marvelously portable. I have a painting-sculpture-design background and after marriage and two babies in rapid succession I found it impossible to paint and sculpt in a small apartment . . . it was natural to gravitate to textiles. Fibers are such that they can be dropped to attend to a crying baby and resumed easily. I remember those endless hours in doctors' offices, traveling by car or plane, etc., that were put to good use with needle or knot.

The nature of stitchery is non-exclusive. You are free to talk and listen as you sew. Telephones and typewriters are exclusive—using either machine tends to cut off communication with other people. Children sense this very fast. I'm still amused to find that if I call a mother of small children, a crisis often ensues at the other end of the line. If ever children are going to scrap and scuffle, it will most certainly be while mother is on the telephone (full volume, at her feet). Unfortunately, this tendency to feel excluded does not disappear quickly. Even teen-agers (and husbands, for heaven's sake) always have the most urgent questions while you're on the phone.

When you are working in fibers it is often possible to sit down with a child and give him your full attention. With appliqué, for example, if the composition is arranged, you can sit and sew and listen to all the details of why the opposing team won the ball game or what Suzie's mother said about women who work. This has always been one of the beauties of hand-sewing. It puts the other person at ease. He need not say anything important or anything at all, for that matter, and it won't waste your time. But your presence, with only your fingers actively involved, lets a child know that you are ready to talk or to listen, without any obligation to talk on anyone's part. And listening is one of the most important things that any one person can do for another.

Child care *does* require quantities of time, work, a sense of humor and a perspective on long-range goals. The question is—can professional work and child care co-exist? Can you quilt in the nursery or have a playpen in the studio? It is possible to find a balance, gaining satisfaction from each—but it takes a lot of juggling, planning, flexibility, and just plain doggedness.

I have seen many women allowing their children to take over their lives (in a negative way). I think it's very important to teach children to amuse themselves, to do for themselves, to respect others' time, space, and being. I must say that all my friends with young children seem completely overwhelmed and unable to find any time for themselves. Once the kids are allowed to become little tyrants, there seems to be no way out of it! (Designer and artist)

To stem the fear of losing myself in the 24-hour demands of raising small children, I hired a summertime A.M. baby sitter and retired to another part of the house to weave. This was the best investment in myself I could have made and everyone in the family is much the better for it. (Nancy Papa)

I know many women who devoted themselves to their children and were suddenly cast aside when the children were grown up: I say that they have nobody to blame for that but themselves. If you depend on your husband and/or children for your own identity, what are you left with when they are gone? I'm just feeling my way along this road, and I don't mean to sound self righteous. I just feel that you can make time for anything that is really important to you, and that fulfilling yourself and developing your own inner resources and inner beauty is crucial. (Karen Jahncke)

One of the girls came up to me one day all excited and said, 'Mommy, thank you for washing my green panties.' Then it hit me, that I had never, in all those years, ever thanked my mother for doing my laundry. (Rivkah Sweedler)

To me homemaking and raising children are a very exciting part of a woman's life, not to be looked upon as a chore but as a challenge. This is when the use of creative ability works at its best. It is an exacting job for which most women have virtually no training; it is a learning on the job situation. I was in no way prepared for it. (Jacqueline Enthoven, author, lecturer, craftswoman and designer)

"I make an effort to maintain a healthy balance between what I do for my children and what I do for myself, to keep any guilt feelings or frustrations down to a bare minimum. In times of conflict I remind myself that in a hundred years my current problems will not be important."

Momo Nagano (Photographer: Maria Kwong)

5.
Coping With the Mess

"I was the first and only girl in my junior high class to get a 'D' in Home Ec. My teacher even suggested to my best friend that I wasn't a suitable companion since I would never be a home-maker. But I persevered. I taught myself to sew and it has been my main passion every since."

Reta Miller (Photographer: Robert Koval)

More than one person's interest is at stake when a woman/mother/wife attempts a career that takes nearly total commitment. In my case, happily I can say that my husband realizes my need to be an artist and supports me in every way possible. (Madge Copeland)

If my husband didn't like the mess I'd leave him, because he obviously wouldn't love me. (Peggy Ritsi)

My husband likes the activity and the mess of my work. It adds a whole new dimension to his life. (Elsbeth Ramos)

A serious craftsperson must have a supportive spouse—those who don't either split or one or the other of them lives in frustration and anger. If my husband didn't like (or at least tolerate) the mess and activity, I couldn't be a weaver—in fact would not have become one in the first place. I came to it after we'd been married for several years, bought my first loom with his blessing. He even took it apart, loaded it on top of the car and brought it back to Illinois from Gatlinburg, Tenn. He's been very supportive and most tolerant of the mess—to the extent that he will do surface cleaning if it's bothering him. (Sharon Lappin Lumsden)

Husbands are alternately understanding or irritated. Mine scolds us about paint brushes or glazes in the kitchen sink, pins hidden in the rug, papers and drawings littering the work bench, or the portable loom in front of the TV. He's right, too. Some glazes are poison and you can't see the football game through the loom. (Carolyn Vosburg Hall, from her "Art and the Kitchen Sink" in Working Craftsman*)*

•

The very existence of messes is a debatable issue. Like beauty, they exist in the eye of the beholder. One sees what another does not. What appears to be reasonably well-ordered work-in-progress to one person may be interpreted as an incredible mess by someone else.

Mess suggests a loss of logical order or a disruption of customary procedure. In that sense every home has some messes, at least some of the time.

A mess can develop from any of the great variety of sources. Some messes occur from the overlapping of different kinds of work (making felt over the kitchen stove, for example). They may also occur when no space has been designated for certain kinds of activity (sewing on the dining room table for lack of studio or sewing room). Messes develop when some activities must be postponed, even temporarily, for others (dirty dishes accumulate because clay is drying or a deadline is approaching). Messes also result when schedules get scrambled, family plans overlap, and household traffic becomes congested.

When a room has a distinct function and activities remain within the boundaries of that function, there is seldom any problem. A kitchen used solely for cooking and a studio used exclusively for weaving are readily acceptable. It is yarn-dyeing in the bathtub, kids lunching in the sewing room, drawings spread out over the dining room table, and sports sections or funny papers obliterating the typewriter that prompt conflicting attitudes to emerge.

Women actively exhibiting and producing in fiber arts have already resolved most of their conflicts relating to mess. Many husbands are supportive of their wives' interests, talents, and creative drives and are either unconcerned with or adjusted to the accompanying jumble. Those women have little need for this chapter, which describes how some fiber artists handled difficult situations and offers comments that reflect their attitudes about the problems. However, any woman encountering conflict over the presence of her creative clutter may find this chapter essential to civility and survival.

If, in your partner's view, surface clutter is intolerable and tidiness has greater significance than your creative needs, you have several alternatives. First, you can give up your own creative work completely (as many women have) for a perfectly kept household. This will probably leave you feeling frustrated and resentful. Second, you can give up any semblance of an orderly home and devote all energies to your art. This will probably leave your husband feeling resentful and you feeling guilty or uncomfortable. Finally, you can search for some balance between home maintenance and creative work. This requires flexibility, co-operation, good humor, and compromise from both yourself and your partner. You will need help from your family and perhaps from outside the family.

Everyone has some idea of what "the good life" should be like, and of the patterns our daily lives should follow. Our own expectations will not necessarily parallel those of other family members. Carolyn Vosburg Hall writes that her husband

has a clear idea in his head of how an executive should live—neat house, well-cared-for-kids, well-run parties, well-handled entertainment, and a home that's a haven from the pressures of the outside world. And in general I agree that that's a very nice way to live. I envision all that too plus being a serious artist. The only part where we disagree is that I don't like being the one who does all that. But that is what I chose . . . so the only solution is to work out compromises. Pay some good cleaning help to keep up the house, convince him that I am a greater asset as an executive wife with another career. It's true that I scare the other wives, but it is wrong in my mind to be less than you can be. Over the years we have worked it out. During the day I am an artist. Evenings and weekends I pay more attention to being the Mom.

If you encounter problems with the Mess, you may really be coping with attitudes about a second career within the family. The physical aspects of disorder (the loom, the yarns, or the quilting frame) are relatively easy to handle. It is the disorder in the pattern of day-to-day living that is more difficult to deal with.

The clutter of fabric, fiber, or paint is superficial. An objection to their presence often indicates an objection to something more basic, beneath the surface. The existence of a woman's career, of her absorbing or passionate involvement in her own work, may be the real source of disturbance and complaint.

Our energies are often expended in dealing with the reactions to disorder more than with the disorder itself. If a husband gets upset when work is left out, the disorder and clutter simply provide something visible and tangible to which criticism can be directed. His annoyance may indicate he feels left out or that he is actually resentful of his wife's dedication to her work. Or he may consider his need for an orderly, tidy house to be of greater importance than her need for creative work. He may feel that, having worked hard all day, he deserves peace and tranquility when he gets home. Whatever the source of the critical attitude, it's time to talk about it and try to work out reasonable plans and compromises.

Barbara Murdock describes her husband's reaction to disorder:

He supports me in my endeavors—but I drive him crazy with my clutter, mess, threads on the floor, needles and pins inbedded in the carpet! He is a compulsive neatnik and cleaner. (Can you imagine being followed about by a man with a sponge and broom?) He has, heroically, made a lot of adjustments through gritted teeth. The house is usually chaotic until 3 p.m. at which time Cinderella turns into a human dynamo of vacuuming, sweeping, cleaning, picking up, which is o.k.—because I am not functioning creatively after that time anyway.

Not all husbands adjust, and some women find they *do* have to make a choice. If you are faced with inflexible attitudes you may be forced to decide what is most important. Eleanor A. Van de Water has expressed her position this way:

I need intensity. I thrive on that. I have a tremendous need for creative expression. I could not survive as a person without it. If I got to the point where my husband could not accept that, and we may be arriving at this point, my instinct for self preservation and identity would be the strongest instinct.

Particia B. Foley adds:

If my husband didn't like, or at least tolerate, the activity and the mess, we would not be married. Wives have been so conditioned to accept the confusion made by husbands (working late, out-of-town trips, transfers, and so on) and learning to cope with it all gracefully, but most men have not been conditioned to do likewise for wives! And so many women seem to think that is the way it should be. I haven't burned my bra; I am not a woman's libber. I am in favor of people, men and women and children too. We all should be given the chance to grow as much as we can. If I encourage my husband and son to grow, should they not do the same for me? That is not a gift, that is a right!!! of all people.

Activity and involvement do create clutter. Nobody works in fibers without creating *some* mess. With a home studio your work is going to be right there underfoot. The degree to which the energetic disarray is tolerated will reflect attitudes of the artist and her family towards her work. The amount of chaos may also reflect the artist's needs for space, storage, and time. Most of all, it offers a clue to the importance of her creative pursuits. But the mess may be only the tip of the iceberg. Beneath the littered surfaces lie the fiber artist's creative energies, talents, and aspirations. So a response to the artistic clutter is a complex one.

You may be able to stand the jumble of your materials while you are working but not your family's reactions to it. Remember that when you are involved in a professional pursuit, there simply will be less energy and fewer hours per day available for picking up and putting away, for dishwashing, for making beds, for dusting. While a family may "put up" with the mess, it is usually the woman who copes with it. Frequently she herself is the one who feels agitated, guilty, and compelled to clean it up.

The mess or clutter that results from inadequate work space can often be resolved through physical changes in space. Adding a studio is ideal, but if this is impossible, try a table or desk for a start. Chapter 2, "Finding Space," deals with the problem in greater detail. But it does help to remember that if a shortage of space is the difficulty, the problem is not entirely yours. Most homemakers do not *choose* to have messy homes—the messes are simply the result of other choices. One crafts-woman says, "If my husband didn't like the mess I'd probably say I didn't like all the mess either and what should *we* do about it. If he is asked to help solve the problem, then he probably won't complain about the results."

Jackie Vermeer puts it this way:

If a husband objects to the mess ask him to help figure out a better solution . . . build a divider or make some better storage. Involving him will help. At least he should understand the problem better.

Besides, he must have some messy habit himself. I don't think anyone is perfect in that department—a cluttered desk, a messy workbench or just clothes on the bedroom floor. Keep those in mind so that when the problems of messes come up you can tackle them all at once.

Some women arrange their work so as to avoid criticism. Stitcher Maggie Turner says: "I keep my mess in "MY" room so my husband does not complain. He tells me that my stitchery is a good way for me to handle my anxieties: (he's a psychiatrist)."

If you weather the disruptions of your first creative projects with equanimity, your husband may adjust, like quilter and teacher Doris Hoover's:

Husbands mellow—at least mine has. An immaculate house isn't as important as it was when we first married (26 years ago). However, his being a traveling man has helped; when he's gone I spread out all over the house and leave it till just before he comes home.

Since most households consist of two or more persons (anyone living alone is probably not encountering the same difficulties in getting it all together), the problems of mess are rarely confined to the person who creates them. In any home involving you, a husband, children, partner, parents, or relatives, multiple needs and interests have to be considered and met and multiple "messes" dealt with.

One of life's greatest joys comes through sharing it with another adult. We all need someone to hug and reassure us when things go badly, to celebrate with us when they go well. Warmth, love, encouragement, and support are vital in the relationship between two people—each needs to give them and to receive them in a comfortable, healthful ratio. But encouragement and support for the fiber artist involve recognizing the importance of her creative drives and then encouraging the diligent (and sometimes passionate) pursuit of her craft. And tolerating the ac-companying mess! Supporting her efforts suggests a sanction of the creative milieu. Lip service to the importance of creativity does not co-exist with demands for house-keeping perfection. Individual needs as well as mutual needs must be discussed. Ways of handling messes will grow out of an understanding of needs.

Mess is not usually the *cause* of home problems—it is the factor that triggers reactions, indicating underlying attitudes towards the woman's creative efforts.

Of course, not all fiber artists have husbands or partners or roommates. Some women, by separation, divorce, or widowhood, are led to a return of single status, though often with children. Others make an early decision to remain single, consciously and deliberately, it terms of artistic or career needs. Those women do not face the same problems of feeling guilty for messing up someone else's home space.

Dee Mosteller comments on her single status:

When I was eleven years old, without any reason or environmental stimulus, I announced to my best friend, Trula Greenhill, that I was going to be a writer. A practical commitment began . . . when at age twenty-nine I said good-bye to a commercial writing job cum magnificent salary, fancy expense account and swell office, and went home to an empty refrigerator, and knew I had to produce to live, both physically and mentally.

That commitment, from age eleven on, did indeed affect my decisions regarding marriage and family. It made me much more careful in seeking a mate who would encourage me, or at least let me alone with my decision. As a result, I've never married, although I've had some very good, stable relationships with men throughout my life.

Once the importance of your own work is understood and accepted, then messes are relatively easier to handle. A short discussion often solves issues of mess before they become serious. Since your total immersion in your work may leave the family feeling temporarily abandoned, talk to them, explain deadlines or priorities, prepare them for what's to come. The labyrinth of yarns and fabric, the actual creative clutter, is more difficult to tolerate than the theoretical mess, so start with the theory. Allow time for everyone to get used to the idea: they will be better prepared to step through the maze. Much fiber work is sporadic. Deadlines are met and there's a relaxed time to tidy up. An exhibit opens, and the chaos at home is put in order. Families find it easier to accept your involvement for a set period of time.

While relatively few women with whom I talked had chosen to remain unmarried, there were more who chose to marry but decided to remain childless, and many who carefully limited the number of children to either one or two. There is little doubt that in reducing the number of people involved, the complexity and chaos is also reduced.

In any living arrangement where a woman is the homemaker (especially if there are children), both partners must desire the woman's career if their lives are to proceed smoothly. Both must consider her professional or artistic goals as basic and important to their lives. If the partner is against it, he will not help make it possible. And a wife can't seriously pursue her work and have her husband's life remain untouched or unaffected by her work.

The artist whose husband regards her as a whole, vital, functioning human probably encounters few obstacles in pursuing her career. He wants her to explore her talents and abilities as much as he has explored his own (even if it involves disorder). He wants her to have the same satisfactions and joys in her work as he finds in his. While this may sound ideal, it does actually and not infrequently occur.

Husbands respond in varying ways to home studios and second careers in the family. And wives respond to their husbands' responses. Some men are tremendously supportive—not just theoretically, but actually and physically. Rose Dwight says:

My husband is one-of-a-kind. He is the only psychologist I know that isn't crazier than hell. He is very understanding, patient and he can really put up with lots of stuff. He has always been a family man, always done more than his time with the girls. Three years ago, instead of some useless flowers or more fattening candy, his gift on Mother's Day was to wash the dishes for the next 12 years (since I had done them for the most part for the first 12 years). I must say he has never reneged. . . .

The importance of her spouse's support is noted by Madge Copeland:

I don't suppose that I would ever have attempted to develop my art if it hadn't been for his support on all fronts. He has (under duress) allowed me to fritter away our modest income on yarns, jute, and equipment; he has given me lots of encouragement (this is the essential— without that I don't think any woman can really forge ahead—if married); and he's cut boards, drilled holes, nailed, etc. Plus he babysits while I teach, does dishes and makes dinners when I can't. He is a resident in heart surgery with terrifically long hours.

For many it is simply a matter of finding flexible and workable solutions. Compromises develop over the years. All family members become more accepting of others needs and interests. Joyce Aiken comments on mutual compromise and changes in her spouse's attitudes:

My husband does not like disorder—but he likes me and years ago had to make the choice. Once a month I try to invite friends in for dinner. It forces me to clear off the dining room table. The kitchen also gets cleaned and the clutter in the living room shoved out of sight.

Ellen Phillips, an exhibiting artist, found compromises that satisfied both her husband's interests and her own:

Occasionally husband has had it! Last year I got the word that he wanted to eat in the dining room (after six weeks of eating in the kitchen). So I opened up the table to its fullest and each evening moved all of my work to one end. It was a compromise that satisfied him and didn't put me out too much. He does get fed up with the mess occasionally. More often he dislikes it if I prefer to work when he wishes to party, go to a show, invite friends in—so I try to balance this out.

Most families function on a cooperative basis, shifting emphasis and roles as needed, supporting one another. Kathy Vidak, teacher and craftswoman, says:

My husband is fantastic! He realizes how I am and he accepts it. I love my home, children, homemade bread and apple pie, but I have to feel creative in my very own field, too. Sometimes, if it looks kind of hopeless, he'll pitch in and get dinner himself.

When two people enjoy and respect one another, each wants the other to find excitement, satisfaction, and fulfillment. If a husband doesn't like his wife's creative work, it may mask some other dissatisfaction with life or within himself. Not all men do exciting, satisfying and challenging work, and it is as essential to help them find fulfilling work as it is for them to help us.

Men who are dissatisfied in their own work often feel frustration in their personal lives. A man must be mature and secure enough in himself to accept his wife's growth without trying to make her fit his image of a wife, just as a woman must feel like a complete person to nurture and support her family's growth and development.

It is not easy (it is sometimes not possible) to be a part-time artist, since art is a full-time commitment. It is what you are 24 hours a day, and if you spend only five hours a day in your studio, the commitment is still there full time. If creative work is essential to your happiness, then anyone who loves you should accept that and help you find your creative outlets to whatever extent is possible.

Some women say their husbands are supportive but what they really mean is that they do not detect outright hostility. Others note that a feeling of support may indicate that the husband has not yet noticed what she's working on. Support is a loose and sometimes deceptive word which may mean anything from "not actually opposed to" to "wildly enthusiastic." Some women feel supported if their husbands "let" them work. I would never accept the idea of having someone's "permission" to do what I want to do with my own life.

I don't need anyone's permission to be an artist. That doesn't mean I won't discuss it and talk it over, ask for help, criticism, or advice; I need all those things in ample doses. I care about other people and how my decisions affect them. But I must make my own decisions, whether right or wrong. I could not live with anyone who did not regard me first of all as a whole person with my own needs and interests. My husband doesn't "let" me pursue my career any more than I "let" him do his work. I have what all fiber artists require and what most active fiber artists have—real support of every kind whenever it is needed.

I have been helped and encouraged, emotionally and financially. The most important element in this is knowing that someone cares, values my work, glories in my successes, and is ready to console and reassure me if necessary. Without that help I might have survived as a designer and writer, but it wouldn't have been anywhere near as much fun.

Soft-sculpture artist Barbara Kensler also feels that

it definitely helps if you have a supportive and understanding husband—in fact, it's imperative. I've always felt so very fortunate to be able to "do my own thing" and not work at a 9-to-5 job every day. My husband's job makes this possible, so I try to show my appreciation by also running a happy, pleasant home. It is a real challenge.

Relationships that allow two people to co-exist professionally do exist. We all know examples or are part of such reciprocally satisfying arrangements. Mutual respect and mutual support are the basic elements. I couldn't really respect and admire or enjoy a man who'd sacrifice his career for mine—and I assume the reverse to be true, too.

I have talked with women who have described to me how they hid their stitchery or craft projects before their husbands came home. The husbands, it seems, wanted immaculate houses and someone to wait on them (instantly!) for dinner. That such men exist does not surprise me so much as the fact that some women will actually hide their work under the bed in order to appear "totally domesticated." Such men might do better to hire a maid. The frequent sad result of such relationships is that after a few years of complying with such demands, these women are often found by their husbands to be exceedingly dull and uninteresting. The husband moves out, smitten by the secretary at work whose apartment is filled with her own paintings or photography, which she *never* puts out of sight.

Some men can very nicely tolerate the mess when they understand its value, and for some, it can be justified by financial gain. One painter says, "What happened to my husband's attitude after my first commission was wonderful to see." Another adds, "The first time I actually got a check for work I sold he quit commenting on my cleaning up. Somehow, that justified it, and gave the work value in his eyes."

And one husband commented to his artist-in-residence wife after her first magazine commission, "You mean they paid you that much to use your dolls? Let's see them again. Now you kids keep your hands off, be very careful . . . this is Mommy's work."

Other husbands find that a wife's creative growth more than compensates for household chaos. And many women somehow manage to maintain a reasonable facsimile of the average American dream home while being full-time fiber artists.

Untidiness in your own home, even when it is agreeable and acceptable to your family, may be the subject of discussion among other relatives or neighbors. If your priorities are in order you can relegate such opinions to their proper insignificant position.

A student recently shared an amusing incident in a weekend extension class. When the noon hour arrived, the few men in the class went out to eat, and the women (who had brought lunch in brown bags) plunked their elbows on the work tables and said, "Okay, let's talk." I suggested that we start out by describing what each had done before she could leave for her 8 a.m. class that day. The answers varied, since we had students from the University, young teachers and mothers, and a sprinkling of older women. The exchange was marvelous and it was especially helpful to the younger women to see that (with experience and age) situations seemed easier to handle. One of the more experienced women offered this:

This morning, just as I was trying to get the kids breakfast, make coffee for my husband, see that lunch was in the refrigerator and gather my class materials, my mother-in-law dropped in. She walked in (gingerly), looked around at the kitchen floor and observed, "You know, Marilyn, over at your sister-in-law's you could just eat off the floor." I looked up and said to her, "Oh, you can eat off the floor here too, you know . . . look, there are some raisins, here are some cracker crumbs, a little dog food and there're some Cheerios."

Housework and the handling of the day-to-day mess of ordinary activity by and large belong to women. And it ordinarily remains that way unless specific arrangements are made to change it. If both you and your husband have put in a ten-hour day at work, the dishes in the sink and the unironed laundry will still, in most cases, be seen as *your* neglected duties. You will have to initiate the changes.

Jo Diggs comments that while her husband "would never dream of fussing about mess, he would never clean it up either. He would never complain about the activity itself because he knows I couldn't live without it."

Another fiber artist, whose husband is also an artist, and who has no children, made this statement:

He's delighted with my endeavors and has always been helpful and co-operative—but not to the extent of doing any of the housework. Several years ago he voluntarily took over all the dishwashing. Probably because we are at a standoff about getting a dishwasher and apparently he would rather do them than get one. He does the yard work; except for dishes I do everything else. No, I don't like it, and I do not think it is particularly fair.

Irene Ferrini-Tuttle sums it up this way:

Choose the right man. One who has respect for your needs—but then don't let the mess and activity go too far. There's a limit. I don't want his business to infringe on our life beyond a point either, so I suppose mutual respect and awareness of individual needs is basic. Usually when I reached those points where my art was consuming the household, he finally screamed, and I realized I'd gone too far and retrenched. However, when I had deadlines, or shows coming up, everyone in the family co-operated and helped with meal preparation, etc.—especially my husband. He is totally disinterested in the process of my work; has never stretched a canvas or made me a storage rack or stretcher bar, but is in other ways very supportive. I have no clues about how one achieves this attitude of support if it doesn't exist. And if it doesn't exist, I see only two outs—divorce or give up one's work.

My husband is a sculptor and works in a studio adjoining our home. We have no set schedules and do our professional work on a free-lance basis. Hours and days run together in our house, unless I'm teaching or giving a lecture. We live around our work. Dinner may be at five or at nine, depending on what's going on. Whoever finishes first starts cooking.

The physical clutter never bothers anyone but me, and I'm doing better every day at not minding. Our biggest messes are always those of timing. One finishes a commission as the other is in the midst of a publication deadline. Free times only occasionally coincide. If we had what relatives describe as "real work" we could plan our vacations together!

Overlapping time commitments are difficult and the problems of scheduling and timing are more intricate when there are two careers involved. These lead to the situations which strain and test the most supportive relationships. Combining career with home is possible, and sometimes each supports the other. The woman who publishes stories which she has written and illustrated for her own children has fused two major aspects of her life. Combining her career with her husband's career is sometimes not accomplished as smoothly. Commitments do not always dovetail. What happens, for example, when she is invited to a preview party or a press opening for her own exhibit and it is scheduled for the same evening as a dinner party with her husband's boss? How such a conflict is resolved will clearly reflect how well a couple is handling the second career in the family.

I've experienced similar situations and I see several acceptable alternatives. One: go to his dinner, leave early, then spend the rest of the evening at your opening. Two: go to your party early and make an appearance after dinner. Or you can each attend your own function. I certainly would not ask my husband to give up an engagement that was important to him so that he could attend mine. Nor would I care to do that myself. The foregoing choices are all based on the assumption that you both *want* to attend both functions. Another very inviting alternative might be to skip both, stay home, and have your own party.

These situations do require flexibility and willingness to adjust from both parties —they can also be devastatingly revealing in terms of who considers what to be the top priority.

Messes develop, then, from a variety of sources. Defining them requires a value judgment. A husband may say his home life is in a mess, while his wife is excitedly exclaiming over her upcoming show. It is a matter of interpretation and viewpoint. Standards change according to one's priorities. If your work is really important to you, forget the mess. If pleasing your husband's whims about the housekeeping is essential, then you'll put your own interests out of sight and cater to his. If you are lucky, you can both compromise.

When you find satisfaction in creative work, all other jobs will be easier. Housework and "messes" seem to fall into proper and appropriate perspective.

When there are intriguing projects and activities going on on top of the table, most people do not see the fur-bunnies under the table. Friends will be too busy enjoying your quilts or your fabric sculpture to notice your housekeeping. A house as neat and orderly as a motel room brings little joy to anyone, although it may offer security to someone who wants things "set" and "right."

To summarize an approach to messes, then, consider these things. First, if for years you've made it difficult for yourself by jumping to meet every demand made upon you as cook, waitress, wife, mother, mistress, laundress, and housekeeper, you'll have to do preparatory work. Let your family know what's coming. Announce that you're going to be silk screening or working on a quilt and that the dining room table will be off limits for a few days. You can even solicit help in selecting materials. That works pretty well; then the mess is not all yours. Talk to your partner, to your family. Discuss issues openly and *honestly*.

If the mess does become a real issue, discuss values with your husband. Is a clean and orderly house more important than your interests? Should it be? If this becomes a more serious issue, ask yourself if it is the activities and clutter he doesn't like or is it some need of yours which he doesn't want to recognize?

Finally, creative clutter is sometimes frightening or threatening to family members (husbands especially) for whom it may represent competition. If you have been totally devoted to a partner and you are now engrossed in writing or painting, he may feel a sense of loss. It is important in such a situation to consider the other's needs for love, companionship, and attention. When these needs, which all of us feel, are satisfactorily and warmly met, tolerance for the activities comes much easier.

My husband seems only to require a full refrigerator and his toes kept warm at night (both are in my interest too) as part of the lover-wife role. The bulk of my time is mine to commit. (Nancy Papa)

He loves me—what can he say! He doesn't mind the mess. I am enthusiastic about this particular subject. As a teacher I have been responsible for the demise of many clean houses. I once visited an ex-student's house—her family room was a pile of fabric, the fireplace and couch were completely hidden. Her husband said to me, "I have you to thank for this!" but he was laughing. (Reta Miller, artist and craftsperson from Oregon)

Activity he doesn't mind. Mess he hates. Most of the time he is fairly patient about it. My happiest day will be when my work can support—if not me—a cleaning woman. (Jo Morris)

If my husband doesn't like all the mess and activity, liberated woman that I am, I clean up and quit the activity. (I also have worked hard for ERA and NOW. The theory is good.) (Barbara Threefoot)

Sometimes my husband gets upset over the mess. He'll then clean up a path. (Beatrice Sheftel, teacher and artist)

"My husband hates the mess. He is vociferous about it, so gets it out of his system and that's it. It goes on just the same way."

Erica Wilson (Photographer: Vladimir Kagan)

My husband is very tolerant, but at the same time I try not to push things too far where leaving messes around is concerned. After all, it's his house too, and I care what he thinks and feels. (Lynda Lanker)

I think he resents my mess—but I don't think he'd ever admit to me that he didn't like it. I pick up when he resents it . . . but he helps me so much in my work. (Jorjanna Lundgren, fiber artist)

You can clean, cook, and organize your whole life away if you're not careful, and I find I just can not spend all my time doing those same old things I'll have to do again next week. It is depressing and, while I like a relatively neat, well-run house, I feel that I must have something to show for the hours in my day besides just a clean sink and a well-scrubbed "john." (Gloria McNutt, stitcher and doll maker, California)

He encourages my ART work, but is sometimes mystified by our unkempt house. (Maryellen Nix, printmaker)

The only time I really worry about the mess is when Bob has been out of town to a meeting—especially Boston where they must have a lot of tidy people. When he leaves, all projects come out and it is a menu of Big Macs—then we have a Big Clean Up before he returns. When he is here to observe the continuous rise and finish of some big project it doesn't seem to bother him. If I worked constantly or daily it probably would. Also, I'm not the world's greatest house-keeper so any improvement is appreciated. As for activity, Bob has a very demanding job, works a long day as an M.D. and often spends an average of two hours an evening in his "work space" writing, dictating, or reading. I work my hours around his and try to keep all weekends free and open. (Jerrie Peters)

A "must" on my expense list through the years was cleaning help. This was not a luxury—I considered it a necessity and preferred to skimp on other things. My husband has always been anti-mess, anti-clutter . . . when I worked after I was first married I felt there was no reason why I had to clean house, too, if he wanted an immaculate almost hospital-like environment. As a dentist, he had nurses and cleaning help in his office, so my philosophy was to carry that thinking home. It was a matter of training right off the bat. (Dona Meilach)

"My husband does not like disorder—but he likes me and years ago he had to make the choice."

Joyce Aiken (Photographer: Jim Heitzeberg)

70

6.
Shifting Gears

"If you are truly serious you can work anywhere. When my kids were crawling and climbing about they always asked if they could eat what was cooking on the stove or was it my work."

Helen Richards (Photographer: Linda Watson)

Nobody liked it when I started teaching at night. I'd get up from the dinner table and go. The first night when I came home the dinner dishes were still on the table, so I just went to bed. Breakfast was very silent over all those dirty dishes. They were finally convinced that I was, indeed, going to teach for the whole semester—and they just changed. I'd come home and the dishes were all taken care of. They got very appreciative of the fact that I had even fixed dinner! I never thought that would happen. (Crafts teacher)

Shifting the direction of my life is really important to me. I'm going back to school to complete my art degree. I want it and need it more than anything. But I don't know if I can take my family's hostility. (Exhibiting artist and designer)

I have just spent 15 years trying to figure out what I want to be when I grow up! It was wonderful to have my 35th birthday several years ago and at last know!! Some moves forward have been easy but most have been a struggle. My own lack of self-confidence was as much a problem as anything else. But after a whole life of doing things for others it is not easy to shift into another gear . . . . I now feel like I'm in DRIVE and I'm more than ever committed and on my way. God! it will be nice to be forty and smug! (Rose Dwight)

If you're making necessary changes and your family can't stand it, that's their problem—not yours. (Overheard, one artist counseling another)

The changes come over the years. When we were first married, I vacuumed every day and even ironed sheets! Can hardly believe it now. I realized during my thirties—when I was Faculty Wives Vice-President, P.T.A. Secretary, Cub Scout Leader, playing bridge, doing all kinds of art work for organizations, let alone raising four children, plus university doings with my husband—that all I could think about was getting through this sometimes boring volunteer work and back into my studio. I began to say "No." I became liberated. (Barbara Kensler)

While I have been a latent feminist all of my life, it took an accumulation of bathroom cleaning and window washing to help me decide that when I died I didn't want the only thing that could be chiseled on my tombstone to be "Her House Was Clean." Somehow this sounds nauseatingly self-righteous, but it took a lot of years to find a suitable format to permit maximum satisfaction for each of us. (Diana Bower)

•

Change remains one of the few constants in family life. Shifting gears is a procedure which occurs frequently as children grow, but the need for it also occurs as adults grow. The homemaker who wants or needs to make changes will have to make adjustments for her own new directions and activities.

Any change in your role that affects other family members will be noticed. If you make a drastic change, such as going back to school as student or teacher, the need for flexibility is obvious. Either happily or grudgingly, families find that their own activities or schedules must be altered to accommodate you. If your change is less dramatic and you remain at home, it is sometimes more difficult for the family to recognize and adjust to it.

The woman who establishes her identity as a fiber artist before becoming a wife, mother, and homemaker has a definite advantage. She's already in gear. As an artist, she then selectively adds home or husband or family (or all three) to a career that already exists. She has established priorities and may require only change in emphasis.

Shifting roles or emphasis later in life is more apt to meet resistance. The man who marries an artist has some idea of his wife's dedication and interests. The man who marries a woman whose life revolves around him, home, and children may feel hood-winked when she decides to run a course parallel to his rather than to be a satellite. One craftswoman described her family's reaction this way:

My family was indulgent about my needlework as long as it never interfered with their needs. So when I started teaching three days a week all hell broke loose. They thought my time belonged to them, that it was their possession, not mine. I had never known that before. It took a lot of time and a lot of verbal battling to resolve it all, and it's still not what I'd call really smoothed out. But next semester I'm going to start teaching one night class too.

Batik artist Barbara C. Kelley says her husband

resents my immersion in something that cuts him out. Finally, with the help of professional counseling, he has come to the conclusion that he has shut me out of his life by his total commitment to his business life and I have to have something that is worthwhile, satisfying and fulfilling—even if it includes a messy dining room table.

You can't change the course of life within the home without creating a few ripples in the family puddle. When change is not accepted and encouraged (or at least tolerated), it can build resentment. As one craftswoman explained it: "I feel it's unfair—he can have his career and can devote himself completely to his work. And he can still have his family, too. I don't have that choice but I make it possible for him to."

Changes within the family structure offer good turning points for shifting gears. If the youngest child starts school in September, *that's* the time to establish a new routine. If your husband is retiring, that change can provide a time to re-order your schedule too. B. J. Adams made positive use of a family move:

Until about six years ago I worked on many things (volunteer, decorating, clubs, children's and husband's activities); then we moved to Washington. With that move I dropped every- thing but Fibers. I had taught stitchery in California, but now decided that that was all I wanted to do and it has for the past few years taken all of my time. I now teach, do commis- sion work, and exhibit regularly in a gallery and in shows; everything from wall hangings and sculptures through basketry and body ornament.

Diane Bower took the occasion of her husband's starting a business at home:

This alleviated my childcare responsibilities considerably. A surprising bonus has been that each family member has become a more responsible person. Consequently, I am now able to teach full time (textiles and crafts) at our community college and to pursue stitching, spinning, weaving, dyeing, etc. from a far more professional self-image.

An important attribute in creating and growing has been to throw off all of those guilt feelings—guilt about not spending hours in the kitchen cooking spaghetti sauce from scratch, guilt about not living in the station wagon like all the car-pooling mommies, guilt about not coffeeing with the neighbors mornings. Satisfaction seems to swell from deciding what is really important and then not playing at it but becoming committed to it.

A new house presents potential for a whole new approach to the use of space. A new city offers the opportunity to re-order social obligations and daily schedules. The arrival of a new baby is a time to drop less meaningful obligations. For Elsbeth Ramos

The most specific event (if such an event can be pinpointed) in helping me channel my creative energies was the shock of moving from my Berkeley home to a conservative suburban tract outside of Los Angeles, being used to the stimulating atmosphere of a university community and leaving a home and studio which had become the very extension of my being.

It was this move, as painful as it was, which severed the umbilical cord. I was in a state of shock, having never confronted the sameness of suburbia, so that I buried myself in my work and it became my reality, my world, my thread to sanity. I made large environments in the garage of our tract home, fighting for space among the tools, garden supplies, bikes, etc. I decided to take advantage of exhibiting and marketing opportunities in the area and soon found myself in the swim of the Los Angeles art world, developing a confidence I never believed I had in me.

If your family is settled comfortably into a routine and you are the only one who desires a change, some strategy may be required to achieve your goals. While you should meet your own needs, you'll want to accomplish that in such a way that your family can enjoy (and benefit from) your new program. If they can't enjoy it, you'll at least want to keep the disruption at a minimum.

The need to grow, to expand interests, to be part of the world, to develop talents and to contribute outside the home, all these factors motivate women to work. Women pursue their careers for many of the same reasons as men do. But pursuing them at home involves different problems. One young fabric artist and teacher says that when she was first married

I stayed at home and just took care of the house and cooked. My husband, a high-school coach, came home afternoons and I'd here this plunk, plunk of the basketball on the driveway, then the swoosh as the ball went through the basket. Three years later, with a toddler and a baby, I'd be holding one child, trying to fix dinner, and planning how I could get out to the grocery store without the baby to tote along. Then I started teaching an adult education class in the evenings, adding another two afternoon classes a week. I did pieces for exhibit and had an occasional commission. Finally, I had a full-time teaching schedule, an exhibitions schedule to maintain, the children and the home and then one day . . . it hit me. I was rushing dinner, trying to mentally prepare for my evening class, organize the fabrics I had to take with me, get the table set, talk to the boys about school, hug them as needed, get the laundry out of the machine and into the dryer, put dinner on, and feeling all the time both the excitement and pressure of a show coming up. Then I heard that plunk, plunk, plunk, swish. And my thoughts shot back to six years ago. I realized his schedule had not altered in all that time. More children, more laundry, more cooking, more shopping had not affected his time or his schedule one bit. Only mine. I had assumed all those things were mine to do. They weren't our children, they were mine. It wasn't our shopping, it was mine. I guess I did that to myself. I assumed I had to do all those jobs if I wanted to be a full-time craftsman.

She has been idling, adapting her life to family needs for years. Now that her needs have been recognized (at least by her), we're likely to hear a little gear stripping as she redirects more of her energies to her own work.

Taking on a commitment outside the home is often easier than accommodating to a home studio for several reasons. The outside commitment offers a regular pay check to justify the efforts; there is a recognized and established company, university, school, or business with which to identify. The outside job is considered "real work." The home studio, at first anyway, has neither reliable financial return nor prestige to lend it importance. Many people have no realistic concept of what an artist or a writer does. Therefore, shifting from the role of complete home-maker to artist/homemaker may present difficulties.

While most couples can adjust, agree to changes, and share new goals and directions, some fiber artists have found that only separation or divorce allowed them to make the desired shift. Those I have encountered survived the initial difficulties and came to enjoy the challenge of supporting themselves. All gained in confidence by being able to cope. They learned to recognize their own resourcefulness and enjoy their newly discovered abilities. Several found it exhilarating to explore their own new-found potentials.

Other artists have faced a time when they had to choose between their artistic needs and external demands. One woman said it was "like choosing between being myself and being what he wanted me to be." While some found that their marriages could not survive the pressure of another career, others made positive adjustments which allowed the women to grow. A strong male ego is not threatened by a woman's talents or her need to realize her potential. A fragile ego may indicate impending difficulties whether or not there is a second career. Remember that while a woman's art work may be the activity that exposes controversy or conflict, *her art is not the cause of it*.

Assume that you have decided to quit trying to do everything perfectly. You are going to concentrate on the vital areas and let a few others go. What's going to be the initial effect on your family? In all liklihood, no one in your family will notice the change until he is actually deprived of some creature comforts. But don't wait for that to happen. Drastic action is not called for, but action is needed.

Start by talking the situation over with your family. Tell them how you feel and ask their help. Let *them* propose changes. Listen to their thoughts, ask for suggestions on how to meet your needs as well as theirs. If you consider your work in fibers as valid as a paying job away from home, as significant as the housekeeping role, or as important as the work of other family members, then help everyone to see that each of you has a commitment in addition to the one at home.

If all other family members have time for Little League, golf, TV, movies, shopping, reading, and bowling, and only *your* time is filled to capacity with laundry, shopping, cooking, and vacuuming, it's easy to see that more than the house needs to be cleaned up. It is unfair, and your family will be able to see that, though you may have to point it out to them. They do, after all, love you. And you may have encouraged their dependence on you by taking charge of everything and accepting all the responsibility.

Be willing to share responsibilities and allow others to experience that much-propagandized "warm glow that accompanies serving others." As I have stated earlier, people who have taken your services for granted are not going to welcome changes that will affect this arrangement. So, if *you* need change, be prepared for the possibility of opposition. Explain your position, take a stand, and maintain it. The degree of opposition will depend upon your family's dependence on you as well as on how you present your case.

Once you have opened the discussion and explained your feelings (and that is a most important beginning), the communication must be ongoing for everyone's benefit. Wilanna Bristo says

an open line of communication and understanding between all family participants at all times needs to be in operation. It takes a willingness to organize, adjust, compromise, set priorities and the ability to say "no."

Your family will probably volunteer to make some changes during the course of your discussion. When they do, don't let the moment's generosity get away. Produce paper and pencil and write it down. That seals the commitment. If everyone offers to cook one night a week, have each person write it on the calendar. And have *them* write it down, not you. Then they have the responsibility. Once they've volunteered to cook, let them know that cooking includes planning, marketing, setting the table, and cleaning up afterwards.

Then stick to the arrangements. If someone has agreed to do the laundry and then forgets—or doesn't do it—don't take over. Let the supply of clean socks run out and let the barefoot members of the family take their complaints to the new "person in charge." Once you've let others take over certain chores, you'll have to be willing to accept their performances. If the kids agree to pack their own lunches, respect that agreement enough to let them take the responsibility—and that means personal responsibility for forgotten lunches as well. If you step in and take over every time the lunch bag sags emptily, then it's still, clearly, your responsibility. Families learn very quickly that they can be lax, knowing that Mom (ever-aware, all-purpose, always-efficient Mom) will swoop in last minute and take over.

Taking too much responsibility can actually be unfair to your children. When a child is given responsibility, it must be given in complete faith. Too many mothers walk dogs, change the cat litter, or feed the hamsters because children who promised faithfully to take care of their pets simply lost interest and failed to do so. If you take over, you teach your child that his promises don't matter, his commitments aren't serious, and that you will always take care of his interests. It's difficult to give a pet away or sell it or take it to the animal shelter. But, remember, it's not your decision—that's the decision someone else made when he didn't care for the pet. Don't deprive your child of the joy of learning to accept responsibility.

My daughter got a horse when she was ten. At least a dozen mothers told me with secretive smiles that they knew I'd end up feeding the animal since "that's the way it always goes." Not always. It was Lizabeth's horse, and she knew that. She has *never* failed to care for it.

When women ask how I accomplish my work, that's part of the explanation—allowing my children to be responsible for their own decisions. Threats mean nothing at all ("If you don't take care of that puppy I'm going to . . ."). Action is the answer, and has to be taken only once for any child to learn. So, don't shift into reverse. Don't make changes which give you *less* time. As a good mother you must help your children become independent, capable, and self-reliant. You *all* lose if you don't.

If the changes offered or proposed by your family don't seem adequate, have suggestions ready. Ask for what is reasonable and you'll be likely to get a positive response. You might ask, initially, for just one day a week to call your own. Or maybe you'd like family members to pick up after themselves, or to give you an occasional evening free of meal planning, cooking, and cleaning. Once you gain the objective, it is important to keep it. Enjoy the burned spaghetti sauce, or don't wince too noticeably. If kids prepare instant pudding, compliment them on it and suggest that since they are so good at making instant, you have a great recipe for "floating island" next time. Encourage all their efforts.

Offers from the family coupled with requests on your part are two major ways of bringing about good changes. If they are not adequate, let these changes become routine and then discuss additional ways in which the family can help. Be gradual, to make it easier for all involved. Consider your family's needs, of course, but don't neglect your own. Be firm and keep hold of all gains. The shifting process requires flexibility and humor.

If you need space, identify what you want and state the terms. For example, if you're quilting a wall hanging and must use the dining room table, announce that you are going to occupy the table for a certain number of weeks. (Overestimate; when you finish early, everyone will marvel.) When your daily progress is visible, others can observe, perhaps become involved and better understand why it can take so long. But clear the table when you promised—keep your word and you won't be suspect the *next* time you announce a takeover.

Family needs change rapidly and continuously. Anticipate changes and as they occur be prepared to move in to new territory. Plan ahead so that when your son leaves for college, everyone knows his room is going to become a new studio. When your daughter (at last!) gets her driver's license, immediately establish the precedent that she does errands. She'll regard any excuse to drive as a delicious opportunity at first. By the time she realizes that driving does not constitute the ultimate fulfillment in life, the errands will be routine. If your husband joins a jogging group or decides to play squash regularly, that's a good time to sign up for a course you've wanted to take.

Your needs will change too. You may start out very casually, exploring fibers in spare time. A few years later, you have become totally engrossed, and your need to create may dominate other aspects of your life. Or you may be back in graduate school or involved in a co-op gallery. As your needs change, family structures must also change to accommodate to your shifts. But such changes are usually gradual and therefore relatively painless. You take one class, or two units, first and decide next semester to take five units. *Then* it's on to full-time school. Or you participate in a group exhibit at a gallery and later have a one-woman show.

Kaethe Kliot, lace artist and teacher from California, "used to be totally Homemaker."

Art and creative work came after children and home, which meant sometimes postponing things forever. Ten years ago when I opened my shop it became a struggle to select which should be first. With encouragement from Jules, some other things became less important. Slowly the struggle became less and a very different ME emerged. Now that our children are teenagers I can put all my energy into my work. It is somewhat divided between business first, creative efforts second, and everything else between. I feel very strange and good in what I do and find myself sometimes startled over my own enthusiasm.

The relationship between husband and wife is an evershifting one. When children are small, most women are willing to be financially dependent. As children grow older, demands on a mother's time decrease and she can increase the time and energy she devotes to her own work.

Alternatives to all-day homemaking and child rearing are available. There are co-op nurseries, preschools, communal living, shared housing, and many husbands are taking more active part in child rearing and housekeeping. While many of these alternatives are highly successful, others are not yet common. Most fiber artists are living in more-or-less conventional life-styles. So while waiting for a more comfortable and accepting climate for social change, it is still possible to make changes within the individual home. Nancy Wettlaufer writes:

Your question presupposes that women run the household and take care of the children while men go off to work. This was true for us, once, when George was working for G.E. (going crazy) and I stayed home with two babies (going crazy). One of the nicest things about being a full-time crafts family now is that these roles can largely be dropped. We both work at home now and share household and child-care responsibilities. It created quite a stir in the local nursery school to have George show up as a "helping mother." Now the title has been changed to "helping parent." So crafts as a family business can definitely be liberating.

Changes for me have been gradual and I was fortunate to be encouraged and helped all the way. I have a lot of drive and energy and I might have pursued this work without encouragement, but support has made it a greater pleasure.

Rose Dwight was attending a summer craft school when she found she

was truly able to step outside my life and see how I was making it. My children survived very well, so did my husband, and I found I could also make it on my own. The best part of this venture was a chance to look at all the ways I tend to the children—thinking they need so much more fussing about than they do. There were days as I zoomed around in my little VW that I thought my carpool schedule must rival Ethel Kennedy's.

The other thing I did was hire a cleaning woman one day a week. The funniest thing, the kids are quite careful not to mess up—because Mrs. Adams cleaned our house. Long live Mrs. Adams!

It is helpful, important, and sometimes crucial to all artists to have contact with others in their field, particularly when venturing into a new field. Most women feel the need for *more* sharing, more companionship with other women artists, more time to critique their work and discuss their progress. Feedback is helpful to the development of artistic work. When you're exhibiting and showing you are getting response and feedback, true. But that's to finished work and it's often at a conceptual stage that such response is most important. You need someone with a similar, serious commitment to talk with and respond to. Because so much of the actual production work is accomplished while working alone in a somewhat isolated way, the need for companionship, exchange, and discussion accumulates. The need is a valid one, and you should plan for it. In the past, when I was extra busy, this contact and communication was one of the "luxuries" I would relinquish. Now I know that it is an essential, not just a nice way to spend a few hours. There are other things I can more easily do without.

Not only does contact with other craftswomen provide stimulation; it is, as Rose Dwight says, a

time to re-evaluate your own work. When things are getting very ordinary it is good to go some-place that is supposed to be a big deal and find that my work is really ok. In fact you may like to know a little something about your workshop in Cleveland that I attended. I went to the opening lecture/slide show and the next day's quilting workshop. First of all I had a chance to observe other craftswomen and note in a new way that my work was coming along and that I need not feel inferior and apologetic about my stuff. But your presence and your work gave me such "juice" that I actually went home and worked 16–18 hours a day.

Beth Gutcheon also notes the importance of dialogue with other artists:

Once I have established a design, I find it adds a lot of depth to the experience, and to the work, to explain what I am doing and why, to someone who is personally and intelligently interested. Friends and fellow craftsmen can provide this. I think that more women work in a vacuum out of shyness and self-doubt than for lack of people to work with if they really want to find them.

DeLoris Stude, quilter and teacher, who opened a shop at age 60 after "20 years of snatching bits of time here and there to do the thing I loved best—working with my hands," didn't want to give up "the active scene of creative happenings." But at her shop,

Now it all comes to me, and I love it. We share, we labor over projects, we are the better for it. The shop establishes a public place for other quilting people to come for inspiration, small talk and supplies and classes.

Recognizing that we need a change is relatively easy. Figuring out how to accomplish the shift is where we encounter difficulties. In summary, the entire process generally follows these steps: defining your needs and talking about them openly with your family, asking for help, listening to and accepting their offers. If their offers of help do not seem adequate, then asking for further help is the next step. Taking advantage of all changes is essential. And finally, it is crucial that you learn to take care of yourself, as well as your family, and see that *your* needs are also met.

Shifting gears is a natural part of every woman's life. The essential thing is to make *positive* changes, so that your creative work becomes an everyday part of your life. This is not always a smooth process. There are times and situations in which choices must be made. They can't be avoided.

If the changes are difficult, seek help. Talk to other women who have encountered similar problems and examine their solutions openly. Talk to friends. One of the great values in this exchange is that just through verbalizing it is sometimes easier to be objective about your own position. When necessary, seek professional help.

We find it easy to justify keeping an automobile in good running condition through preventive maintenance—humans deserve the same consideration. There are many classes, courses, meetings, and women's groups which may help. There are counselors, psychologists, and psychiatrists. Don't overlook your grandmother or great-aunt or teachers, either. And don't overlook your children. Another generation often has a different perspective or viewpoint which may be illuminating.

Consider that you are worth keeping in running order. You owe it to yourself (and your family!).

Finally, remember that you don't have to be the only one to change, shift, adjust, and make allowances. Other people can exercise their capacities for flexibility, compromise, and change. If you have always given in to other people's needs, it'll be difficult to shift to an emphasis on your own needs. It will not always be comfortable or pleasant—it will certainly not be easy. But sometimes the choices can be made by your family—they need not always be your own.

Ed came from an old world background where his mother slaved to keep the house immaculate. At first . . . [my housekeeping] certainly did bother him and there was a period when it became crucial to our marriage that something be done. I honestly don't know what happened except that it became evident to him that I simply was not going to change and so he has come to accept it and now he has his "piles" too. (Joyce Gross)

The reason your lecture to our guild was so very successful is that you devoted part of it to the problems of women trying to find an outlet for their creative needs and still run a family. I would say it was like we had all had a very good session with our favorite psychiatrist and we all felt so good to know that we were not alone in our frustration. (Carole Austin)

My husband never wanted me to run a business, and I never considered giving it up. When he finally realized that he just accepted it and really, he helps me a lot. (Fiber designer and co-owner of a needlework shop)

My college training is as an occupational therapist. I worked for four years, giving everything to other people, working not for myself. Up until the last couple of years I've been extremely active politically, extremely active in social problems—so this is a very introspective time for me and sometimes I feel quite guilty about just pursuing my creative ability, not contributing financially. . . .
I weave because I need to . . . I need the outlet, the rhythm of weaving. It's a meditative process. It's the one time of the day I can go into myself. My weaving corresponds to where I am. About the money I have ambivalent feelings. What I'm doing is very valid for myself and yet my husband, who's a doctor, is helping other people, he's doing lots of socially valid things. (Rivkah Sweedler)

When a woman (or anyone else for that matter) reaches the point that she is not dependent on the approval of others, then she can take charge of her own person. I think that trying to be sensitive to the feelings of others and especially to the ones you love is so much easier to do when you are feeling good about yourself. (Jody House)

These past twelve years have really been an uphill struggle, at home, at school, and in the art world to prove that working with fiber in all its forms was really a serious undertaking; and that I had the right to devote that part of my life that was exclusively mine to that pursuit. But somewhere in the middle of this busy home of demanding but lovable doctor/husband and four really good children . . . NANCY . . . . does exist and manage to devote many quiet hours each week to creating and towards becoming an artist. Though I have been a closet-artist for years, I have only recently gained the courage to use that word in reference to myself. I have been going back to school the past three years, and hope to enter a graduate program . . . I have also become a weaver and am involved with the whole process from spinning and dyeing to weaving and stitching.

We moved to the country three years ago and built a home in which I have my own room for my work. Along with the move to the country came a change of pace and a clearing of priorities as to how I spend my time . . . a quietude and communion with our beautiful hillside. (Nancy Hoskins)

"I use every minute I have! . . . before the family gets up, when the children are napping, while the family is reading or watching TV. For a couple of hours during the day the children understand that I must work while they play."

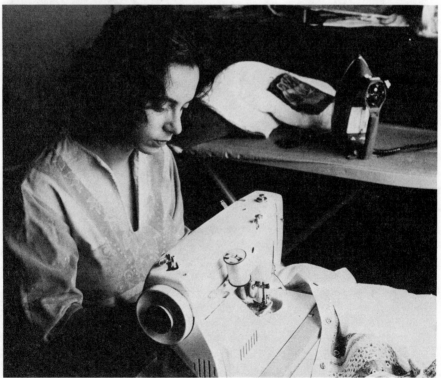

Tricia Klem (Photographer: John Syer)

7.
Getting Started

"Sure you can be a fiber artist and a homemaker! The clue is to take what you do seriously, think of it as work, and believe that you deserve the time and energy it takes. If you refer to it as your hobby, as something to keep you busy, all is lost!"

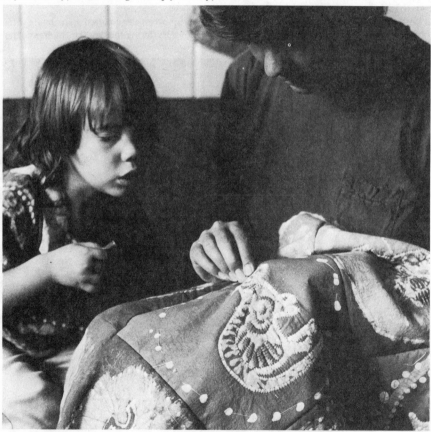

Anne Syer (Photographer: John Syer)

As a student of human nature my ideas come from people around me. Sometimes I have something to say to the world, sometimes a personal message to someone close. Sometimes I just need something to wear to a particular function. (Jody House)

The need to produce is a great stimulation. My work is more of a love affair than a job so it gets the best of me. (Ginny Hoag, stitchery artist and teacher, California)

My formula for the good life is to work at something you really enjoy, and never simply work to feed your face or clothe your back. (Dee Mosteller)

Four things inspired me: need for approval, need for money, support of sharing groups, support of my husband and family. (Jorjanna Lundgren)

I like to think that you can be in charge of yourself, pull yourself out of mental morasses, channel your thoughts to more productive, less self destructive goals. (Carolyn Vosburg Hall)

Ideas come faster the more different media I work in—sometimes they pile up and it's sort of like being constipated. So, I try not to have too many. (Catherine Gibson)

●

Getting started sounds so easy—you just walk into your studio and you *create*. But it is a complex process which does not always flow freely and smoothly and continuously. Children create naturally and spontaneously, and anyone who has retained this ability is fortunate. The rest of us have to relearn the process as adults. We don't all just pick up materials and automatically produce.

Each artist finds certain things that are important in getting started. And since we are at different points in our lives, our motivations, needs, and drives are also at variance. What seems old hat to one may trigger new directions for another. What's obvious to you may be a revelation to me, and vice versa. Yet basic for all of us is the need for a sense of identity, or what is called centering, the need to relate to other people and to our surroundings, and the need to channel our creative energies.

Centering gets an individual in touch, through contemplation or meditation, with the center of his own being, the balance point around which life takes its meaning and assumes form. It is a "homing in" on what is important in life—locating and identifying what is essential, and viewing it in perspective. It puts one in touch with one's relationship to the universe. Centering makes it possible to direct or channel energies towards one's work. The experience varies from one individual to the next —it may be religious, spiritual, or mystical in nature. It may be a philosophic attitude derived from physical experiences. (M. C. Richards' book *Centering* offers valuable insights.)

There are women who find contemplation, Yoga, religion, TM, est, Scientology, relaxation, self-hypnosis, or behavior modification programs an essential part of the day. Use whatever works for you. Any will take time, but may result in a more relaxed, objective attitude towards peripheral activities, helping you to decide what is important in your life. All of this is work. Maintenance details are kept in a comfortable relationship with the more pleasurable creative labors, and your art work comes into focus.

It is no accident that so many women find their artistic centers and creative identities in the fiber arts. Fibers offer continuity and a sense of personal history, since through this art we can further identify with our mothers, grandmothers, and their mothers, and with needlewomen throughout history. The identification has its historical (or vertical) perspective as well as its contemporary (or horizontal) perspective. Needle and fabric arts are practiced and enjoyed by women in all countries and cultures. Our involvement in fibers leads to an increased awareness and appreciation of Belgian lacemakers, Indian embroiderers, Peruvian knitters, Scandinavian stitchers, and our neighborhood quilters, to name only a few. In our own work we become part of this greater community, bonded with women of similar interests everywhere, including the fiber and fabric enthusiasts all over America.

When I quilt I am connected to other women through what has traditionally been a woman's art. When in an exhibit I saw an appliquéd bed cover, made in 1800 by Sarah Furman Warner, I was overwhelmed with the feeling that I knew her. When I sew I am influenced by her love of her village and the people, animals and trees that grew there.

As all of us expand in our own work and explore our potential, we offer our own daughters greater choices. They can connect or identify with us through a variety of role models as writers, teachers, artists, lecturers, designers, or whatever (all interests which grow out of or through our work) as well as the traditional roles of wife, mother, and homemaker.

Fortunately for all of us, a few of our grandmothers never lost sight of the value of these traditional arts. They quilted (or tatted or wove or embroidered) even when their work brought them little recognition and no financial return. But they had other reasons to pursue the work. It channeled creative energies, it was an outlet for the urge to design, to compose, to organize visual elements. They valued one another's work and set their own standards. Obviously the satisfactions were valid enough to keep fiber arts alive when there were few, if any, outside compensations for it.

What motivates women to work in art and particularly in fiber arts is variable, but for many the experience of having small children is related. Motherhood focused Madge Copeland's interests; her work came "out of the frustrations of housewifery and motherhood and piecemeal collected courses several years ago." Barbara Murdock was an art major who

could never really find a niche. Drawing was really my love, but I really didn't know where to go from there. When my last child was born I was at home, nothing much to do and I felt both restless and depressed. I decided to take the evening stitchery class at the University— it was so stimulating! *It changed my life.*

And Jerrie Peters left "a fantastic job" but when she had her second child she found herself

stuck at home with six small children (I babysat to supplement the family income), no money, nor much transportation, and a husband who was struggling through his internship year and never came home. It was either creativity or insanity.

Sometimes insignificant events or happenings strike some responsive note in one's thinking. Barbara Kensler was motivated by an exhibition:

I would have to say, Jean, that seeing your Stitchery Show at the San Francisco de Young Museum in the early sixties was a strong influence on my getting into fabrics. I had painted the previous fifteen years. I was completely intrigued, enchanted and terribly excited about the many possibilities in working with needle and thread. I seemed to know instinctively that this was a medium I must explore. At the time, I was helping put my husband through Stanford by typing papers—it meant a two-year wait before I could really begin my attempts at stitchery but the desire to begin never left me.

Karen Jahncke read books that provided "a sudden release from other people's patterns and ideas" and helped her to see that she "could create my own works instead of imitating or making slavish copies of someone else's ideas." She was

freed in a larger sense after a psychotherapist friend in California made me realize that I was trying to be Super Mom. I felt my duty as a wife and mother was to serve my husband and children, and sacrifice my wants and needs to theirs which I must regard as more important. He helped me realize that by sacrificing myself to them and their lives I was in essence a non-person and would in the long run become a drag on them—who wants to carry the weight of a sacrificial lamb? But, on the other hand, if I was to fulfill myself and develop my own strength, interests and personhood, I would be giving myself and my family a gift more beautiful than anything else in the world. If I am happy about myself and my life deep down, then that is rubbed off on those around me.

As I noted earlier, having some full-time work experience before having a family is a tremendous help in establishing professional identity. It doesn't mean there won't be difficult days. A sick child requires 24-hour care, whether you're professional or not. But having worked alters your attitude about yourself and offers perspective. To some extent it makes you aware of what you can do (or can't do); you can realistically assess your potential, and have confidence in your abilities. It affects your attitude about money: knowing what it is to work for it, you respect it as a measure of time, energy, and ability. And you also know that the work itself has to be worthwhile, that money alone cannot justify a job.

I grew up without much sense of identity, or at least without attributing much value to the identity I had. I did have a passion for drawing and designing, coupled with an utter lack of confidence in my own abilities. I was intimidated by the whole world. I taught school, did a little free-lance work, and took any job— silk-screening theater posters, making someone's Christmas cards, whatever. I approached each job with great trepidation. Success in one endeavor rarely carried over into my attitude about the next. In college I was terrified for days before having to give a ten-minute oral report in class. I have had to teach myself to lecture, and admit that I can now enjoy talking to a group of 200 to 300 people.

Many of us have come to fiber arts by circuitous routes. Even those women whose roles are well outside the traditional ones find some identity in fibers. Their backgrounds vary from painting, sculpture, and design to political science, mathematics, and medicine. There are writers, home economists, and recreation leaders who have channeled their resources into fiber arts. We are comfortable with fibers and identify with them as they have always been related to the home in countless ways. Fabrics and fibers are a part of day-to-day living, materials which are constantly handled and used and with which we are familiar. The current interest in fibers as an art form is significant in many ways: it provides a transition, offering us an area for serious, dedicated professional work while maintaining the more traditional relationship to home and family. The most conventional and conservative fiber artists share interests with those whose life-styles embrace unconventional relationships. It does not seem to matter that there are seemingly enormous differences—they share a common interest in developing their talents and potentials.

The need for a strong sense of identity pervades the work of most fiber artists. The women's movement has helped to make the identification possible. Fifteen years ago when my children were small, I belonged to no women's organizations. I took a certain smug kind of satisfaction or pride in that (it is embarrassing now to admit), as though an organization, simply because it consisted of women only, was automatically of little value. The feminist movement has helped make it possible for me to enjoy women's groups, to realize that they are valid and that it is essential for women to encourage and support one another.

Women are in some ways limited in their means for achieving this sense of identity. Our last names, for example, are not passed on to our children. To get an idea of how important one's name is, check your Yellow Pages to see how many businesses and professions do use a family name. You'll see Wm. Brown and Son, Wm. Brown, Jr., Wm. Brown III, Brown Brothers, Brown and Brown, Inc., and so on.

Women do not have access to this very direct, strong sense of belonging to a continuing line. While this name identity may be on the verge of changing, I still know of no Louise II or Louise, Jr., or Louise and Daughters. Even in this hypothetical example, of course, the first name has to be used since that's the only one that belongs to a woman. Our last names are transient. Our sons will carry on family names and retain their identities, but our daughters, with rare exceptions, will not. They may, at best, face a choice. They can keep their own names (and encounter as I have, surprising attitudes) or they can change their identities.

When I first started teaching and doing free-lance work, as Jean Ray, I felt a sense of pride for my professional name. When I married I added my husband's name. (I didn't know, 23 years ago, that there was any other choice.) Later, when I remarried, I chose to retain Jean Ray Laury professionally.

My present husband once told me that he felt a little odd introducing his wife as Jean Ray Laury. I asked why, since I didn't feel odd introducing him as Stan Bitters. I think he has come to enjoy it. One woman who retained her own name after marriage said that to become "Mrs. Roger HIM" was to assume a name that *anyone* could have had—it didn't refer to her as an individual, only to her husband as an individual. It gave her an identity only in relationship to him.

Every woman needs a strong sense of her own individuality. The name, of course, *does not* prevent a woman from developing that sense, whether the name is hers or her husbands. But it is sometimes difficult for women to have to change identities especially after getting a start on a career or profession.

A name is just one aspect of identity. Fiber artists establish their identities in many ways: being a woman is a basic one; expression through the needle arts is another. As the interests become more specifically directed, the importance of a professional identity increases, as does the identification with other creative artists. Identity then can come through name, sex, and profession as well as through other roles. The woman who is identified as a wife, housekeeper, and mother (all roles that define a relationship) also needs to be an individual in her own right. She must be what Anne Morrow Lindbergh describes in *Gift From the Sea* as the hub of a wheel—a solid person, a center around which family and household activities can revolve. To remain at the center of her own life, at the hub, rather than to end up speeding at the perimeter of others' lives, a woman needs a sound sense of her own worth.

When I first married I felt really relaxed, as though being a wife validated my existence and I no longer needed to *do* something. That lasted a matter of weeks before I knew I had to keep up with my work. But I wanted to pursue it in the security and comfort of my home. I found, however, that there are no assurances of "security and comfort" if you are committed to your work.

Even creative fiber work is not free of risk. It can be challenging and demanding and can make conventional marriage and domesticity look like a very inviting escape by contrast. Offering your work for exhibition or for commissions is hazardous: it makes you vulnerable. If you have only a tenuous grasp on your identity, the risk is even greater. Your work may be rejected. It's certainly *safer* and in some ways more comfortable to just be a full-time wife and mother and avoid the possibility of having your work turned down or criticized or found lacking in some way. Once your statement, whatever the medium, is out there, it can't be retracted. You are exposed. It is a difficult challenge which requires both spirit and daring, and develops confidence. If you don't risk the possibility of failure, you miss the potential for success.

Some women feel confined at home and this prevents them from getting started. But the sense of frustration at being tied to home and children is often a matter of attitude. Sally K. Davidson, designer and craftsman from New York, points out that although she is "somewhat confined to my house in a physical way, and am on a limited schedule, my mind is not confined. Everything around me is interesting and I have a 'pipeline to the world' via my bookshelf and my mail box." And Beatrice Sheftel says, "Even when my son was newborn I was never confined. I don't drive, but I can walk. I'd push his carriage to the library." Jackie Vermeer adds that "It's important to get out to see things. Take children with you (if there is no way to go alone)."

Many women who feel an urge to make a pot or a quilt are afraid to try. I have heard, over and over, "I'm not talented," "I don't have any training," "I never could do that." Nonsense. You can do just about anything you want, if you want to badly enough. Any library has an abundance of books that offer information on every conceivable project: the "how to" is readily accessible. Mothers have always made toys for their children, even with minimum tools. Our grandmothers and great-grandmothers made quilts—they spun yarn, made dyes, wove fabric, knitted, embroidered, and engaged in an endless series of productive, creative activities. We all need such productive, creative work, the opportunity to be expressive. Everyone can be creative in some way—in many ways.

Don't be overwhelmed by experts. Everybody starts out simply and easily and progresses gradually to the complexities, step by step. Almost all talents and skills develop one step at a time. Fine cooks don't learn their art all at once. If you are completely new to herb cooking, you begin with the familiar. You already know how salt affects taste, so you are on your way. Pepper, parsley, and paprika add flavors too, as well as color. You add bay or oregano or rosemary, using each until you know it. Pretty soon you know a lot about herb cooking. Books and cooks may guide you or direct you, but cooking is ultimately a matter of taste. And your taste buds are as numerous and functional as anyone else's. Trust your own judgment, based on experience. Accept what the experts have to offer, be open to their experience, but don't accept their tastes as a substitute for yours.

A complex, intricate quilt design may so dazzle you that you are overwhelmed and immobilized. But remember that the quilt was probably *not* that quilter's first attempt. Try a simple pattern, stripes or blocks of color. When that's easy to handle, move on to another step. Many projects which seem complicated are not really difficult—they just require care and time.

It's important to allow yourself time to learn. Don't make unreasonable demands on yourself. If you were studying drawing, you'd be willing to work for a year or two before you expected to exhibit your work. In fibers, women seem to feel that they should be immediate experts. They enter a first fiber effort in a show and are disappointed in rejection. They would not expect such incredible results from any other art form. So be fair—allow yourself time to learn. Don't underestimate your abilities—and don't underestimate the fiber medium. "Today, many people want instant success, right now!" Jacqueline Enthoven says. "Too often this brings about failure and frustrations which are reflected in attitudes towards the family and more failures."

The ability to keep things in perspective is critical during the years when you are getting started. Work can remain uppermost in *importance* even when it's impossible to lavish all your energies on it. Centering on the most important elements of your life keeps your purposes and goals clear.

A question encountered by all artists and designers is "where do you get your ideas." We are constantly being asked where the inspiration comes from, how ideas develop. When you are clear in your own mind about what is essential, ideas tend to multiply with rabbitlike speed and ease. All you need is one pair to start with. Resource material and inspiration are everywhere.

When one has incentive and purpose, she is motivated and inspiration follows more easily. Invention and originality develop from a variety of sources. Imaginations are stimulated by any of myriad factors in the environment: wind or rain, sand or snow, ferns, weeds, lichen; by the concepts of growth, birth, change, metamorphosis, decay; by people, children, comments, thoughts and the efforts of other artists in music, poetry, painting. Diverse needs are met through this creative work, including those for recognition, expression, identity, self-knowledge, income and success.

Our surroundings are alive with ideas. We live in a continuous deluge of images, visual stimuli and inspiration. Each artist is literally bombarded with ideas which she views through the multicolored lenses of her sense of self, her values or judgments, past experiences, perspectives, and successes or failures. Experiences of every kind pour in a never-ending stream into a receptive mind and come pouring out in creative efforts. It is what happens to the stimuli while they incubate, the selecting, sorting, and organizing, that makes work vital and personal.

Ideas come from what you are and where you are. They grow out of your everyday life, and from those aspects of living that are important to you. Self-study helps define your interests, and makes you receptive to the endless parade of ideas by which we are all continuously surrounded.

Some fiber artists are motivated by practical needs, other are inspired by music or nature. For some, ideas develop out of a playful use of materials and the involvement in one project leads to the next. These are individualized responses, and the comments made are as varied as the artists themselves.

Practically everyone has access to a public library, and books provide one of the most extravagantly diversified sources of visual material imaginable. For Rose Dwight,

The biggest source of ideas has been books. Dayton is not a cultural center—it is a huge industrial center where they make car batteries and air conditioners for farm tractors, where most ideas of art would be a really neatly done paint-by-numbers and the craft world consists of decorated clothespins. But I have been around a bit and I have always been a bookworm so I spend one or two times a week at the library.

All kinds of things keep my mind alive—African repetitive designs, books on Scandinavian design, craft magazines. I don't think it is essential to hop off to New York every other week, but one has to have inspiration. After all—other professional people and most men have conferences and input sessions.

Mary Ellen Hritz, weaver and craftsman from Ohio, adds:

Inspiration and ideas come largely from my friends who are involved in art, and from books and magazines. . . . The library is the greatest source. . . . I try to study at least one book a month on design or related fields.

For other fiber artists it is an involvement with the work itself which gives rise to new directions. Momo Nagano says, "I weave pretty steadily, and the work itself generates new ideas. I have several pieces going at the same time so when one looses its momentum, I can turn to another with a fresh viewpoint. It all sounds good on paper."

Barbara Murdock, teacher and quilter, finds that new materials as well as projects-in-process are inspiring:

Some projects begin in a fabric store—and the fabrics or colors and prints suggest something to me. When I am "poor," I go through the hall closet and spread everything out on the floor.

Other times I sketch ideas to begin with, but really never use them when I begin.

When I am really stuck—I get out an unfinished project and start to finish it—during this process I never fail to develop an idea for something else to do—and I know I will never run out of unfinished projects."

Sometimes inspiration comes from the most mundane surroundings and activities. Ethel Jane Beitler, stitchery artist from Texas, states:

Life is never dull for lack of inspirations and ideas. Even a glass of iced tea, a slice of cantaloupe or a strawberry, blades of grass, a bone from last night's dinner—all give never ending sources of ideas. As one student told me, "I even see designs in my dishwater now!"

And Ellen Phillips adds:

Lately I have found inspiration everywhere—books, found objects, machines, magazines, materials, skyscrapers, automobiles, hiking boots, words, purses, museums, themes, science, music. Creativity seems to need nothing more than an open state of mind and feeling, a wandering eye, touching fingers and love of life.

Another very important source of inspiration and ideas is exchange and communication with other artists. Jorjanna Lundgren notes that "fiber work is ordinarily solitary. Sharing offers tremendous food . . . . your community is what's important; family, church, crafts people, the ones you relate to."

Cathy Ryan feels that

Best of all is to keep in touch and talking with other people involved in the crafts. The insight and support you can get from someone who knows what it means to be committed to developing a craft is invaluable . . . it's the kind of contact that stimulates the creative processes and keeps you going when the work gets to be a bit much.

Eleanor A. Van de Water adds, "There is a kind of gift we can give to one another . . . by believing in someone else's ability and letting them know the extent of our faith and trust in them as fiber artists."

Another artist/designer offers these thoughts regarding a stimulating source of ideas:

My inspiration comes from constantly being in contact with women in my same field doing the same kind of work, from seeing their work, craft shows, other crafts. I very much need personal contact with other people. It is essential to my well-being as a person. I cannot be caged-up in my workroom eight hours a day without other human contact. I guess this is why I am so in favor of things like craft guilds and craft classes. It is so exciting to see how inspiration is generated within a group of people all interested in the same thing. It is so important for women to get together in this way. We all need fuel for our own creative fires and I feel there is absolutely none in the ordinary household with the everyday monotonous chores.

Many artists have to contend with a superabundance rather than a scarcity of ideas. Kitt Heidel, needlework teacher and administrator from Michigan finds "Inspiration and ideas are only problems in that I will never have enough time for all of them."

Carol Cheney Rome is also brimful and adds that

Ideas flood my mind all the time. Many of the inspirations are related to money making projects, such as new book titles, new workshops, etc. However, I also have an idea file for designs and I see design all around me.

She further finds that certain needs serve as inspiration for her work:

I consider myself a decorative artist, or a designer, as my work is usually planned to fit into an architectural setting, and is to be used as upholstery, or whatever. I can sketch quite well, and my photography is improving. My actual work is usually representational—I lean towards plants a great deal. My work is also tight—it might loosen a bit more with more time for experimentation and pieces that are done for the hell of it rather than for some specific purpose.

For Doris Hoover and Nancy Papa, the challenge is that of solving a particular problem. For the one, "Filling a specific need: empty wall space, mending or altering clothing—these are motivations. Inspiration comes from nature, scripture, craft and folk art books and materials themselves"; while for the other, "The problem-solving challenge plays a big part in selecting what I will actually do."

Ideas must be generated from within yourself, but external things can trigger them. Inspiration often just involves a fresh look at the usual or familiar things. It requires effort, and at the same time, originality is difficult to avoid. I have sometimes worked with design classes in which I have asked each member to slice an apple in half and to render it as faithfully as possible in fabric appliqué. Students usually assume that the class will produce a series of identical pieces of work. There are never any two alike, for each student makes her own interpretation as she transfers the image into her fabric. Some see the apple as a full round form, in which the seed core is incidental. For others, the apple is merely a casing for the essential aspect of the fruit—its seeds. Each person envisions a different shape, emphasizes or exaggerates different aspects of the fruit, ignores what she considers non-essential, and interprets the surface in a different way. In this sense, it is impossible to *avoid* originality. It is a by-product of a direct and simple approach. It is the conscious attempt to be original which often produces the least personal and most uninteresting work. So any object can serve as a point of departure; and once the individual is involved in the work, new approaches and ideas develop naturally out of the process itself.

Inspiration and ideas can come from the most ordinary things which surround you. Kitchens are endless sources for design . . . artichokes, peppers, leeks . . . all can provide the springboards from which images or abstractions rise. It often helps to mentally disassociate an object from its function. That frees you to see form without being limited by its intended use. I looked at crocheted doilies for years without ever seeing anything but doilies. Finally I was able to look at one as if it were a line drawing, and a whole new world appeared to me. I had been limiting my view of those delicate traceries and patterns because I could not perceive anything past their functions.

It is often very enlightening to look at forms or shapes, objects or paintings which you don't like or don't respond to. When you attend shows or exhibitions, for example, don't spend all your time in galleries where you like the work. Very often, work you like bears some similarity to your own in color, concept, media, or style. Look at something you fervently *dis*like and try to analyze why you dislike it, or what's wrong. You'll learn a lot more that way.

If you don't like someone else's composition or design solution, figure out how you would handle it. Look at another artist's work and try to figure out where she has been and where she is headed. Your ideas will shoot off in new directions.

Keep a notebook or sketchbook with you at all times. Write notes to yourself, make sketches, jot down ideas. Addresses, drawings, great inspirations, and good recipes may mix on the page to good advantage.

91

Take advantage of every situation. If you're stuck in traffic, design an appliqué for the billboard you're facing. This kind of exercise will develop new ideas or new ways of working. See if there is some pattern in your surroundings (the buildings, heads in car windows, license plates) that lend themselves to a quilt pattern. Don't worry that you won't see the red light turn green—one to six lanes of horns will let you know soon enough.

You don't always have to work directly with fabric or fiber—just visualizing the process gives you tremendous practice. Suppose you want to learn to cut fabric directly, without relying on a drawing or pattern. Practice while you're on a bus: visualize the process of cutting, experiencing it over and over without wasting any material at all.

Evaluate everything you look at in terms of design and pattern, determining how you would make it different. A whole *world* of experience can be chalked up while you're shopping for groceries or waiting at the dentist's. My typist once returned from the doctor's office with sketches for quilt block designs that were developed from the wallpaper in the waiting room!

You'll soon develop the habit of taking visual cues from your surroundings and developing them into design possibilities. Exercise that capacity. It gets easier and more enjoyable, and it's certainly profitable in visualizing ideas and designs.

For me, home offers tremendous resources for ideas. The concepts I enjoy working with seem to spring up out of everyday activity, from garden and woods, from foods and children and books. But different women need different kinds of resources. Home activities can be so demanding that many women simply feel depleted in a home environment. Everyone must seek whatever reservoir will replenish her, artistically and spiritually. That source will vary from one individual to the next.

There's no better place for incubating ideas than in the routine of housework—what a time for thinking and planning and letting ideas percolate to the top. (Jane Chapman)

I can get a great idea while washing the dishes. When my daughter was a baby and I read to her a lot, I obtained ideas for my small embroideries from her books. Ideas also come from the subconscious and I have found that to bring them to the fore, the only requirement is a certain amount of relaxation. Ideas come to me when I'm with the family, by myself, and sometimes teaching. (Wilanna Bristo)

When my girls were being born, I was so busy washing, feeding, running errands that I just kept a notebook of design ideas. This later proved useful. Childhood illness of my second daughter took all my energy for about eight years and drove me to despair. I surfaced from that understanding that I must work on my work, and that worrying over her was only holding her back in her struggle to live and grow. So I turned my back on fear and worry and set to work. . . . That set my life in motion. (Elizabeth Fuller)

Some days I'll get an idea and it will just snowball. Other days, I couldn't remember my name if I hadn't had it for thirty years. (Kathy Vidak)

The whole business has been at once terribly exciting, ego-building, frustrating, aggravating, time-consuming, etc. I have always been torn between who or what comes first—my husband's wishes, my home's condition (it hasn't been carefully cleaned since the magazine was started), my own personal desires to create in a number of craft mediums, being creative in the kitchen, or the demands of answering the steady flow of mail that always brings problems of one kind or another.

This will give you an insight into the way many women like myself feel when they are pulled in several directions at once (most usually by their own choice, I might add) and try to do more than they are capable of doing, as regards their time and energies. (Barbara Brabec)

About three years ago my husband decided to leave the world of big business and follow his dream of teaching in a small college. The resulting drastic salary cut then, plus inflation since, were certainly motivation to work seriously at what I enjoyed most anyway. I was also tired of board meetings, committees, etc., and ready to re-order my priorities. (Joyce Richards, artist, Illinois)

My husband helped me to see that I shouldn't feel guilty if everyone didn't always have clean socks, etc. —that I owed time to myself (when my three boys were in their teens and at home).
  These people inspired me:
  Jean Ray Laury, when asked "How do you find time to stitch?" said, "You have it backwards, it's how do you find time to cook, wash, etc?" As obvious as this may seem—it was a heavy thought for me because it allowed me to turn my priorities around.
  Susan Morrison told me she tries to set short term goals for herself each day. This was an enormous help to me as I tend to think in whole completed projects.
  Joyce Aiken said, "Let the beds go unmade, stop procrastinating and go up into your studio and work."
  The phone company helped: they removed my studio phone bell so I can't take incoming calls but can dial out.
  My husband helps by encouraging me to buy anything I need for my work and thinks everything I do is a masterpiece—even when I know it isn't." (Carol Martin, artist and designer)

I guess the real lesson to be learned . . . is to accept this need to be creative as a duty, like any other occupation. It is not unlike a relationship, growing and changing all the time. One must practice at being open in order to receive the inspiration which is truly a gift and comes with inner contentment. The reflection can only be as pure as the mirror. (Barbara Neill)

"You should have a room or work area that is strictly your own and where you can work without interruption. This should be strictly off limits to children and husbands unless permission is granted. I think it is more productive to have a few uninterrupted hours without children underfoot than a whole day trying to combine motherhood with work."

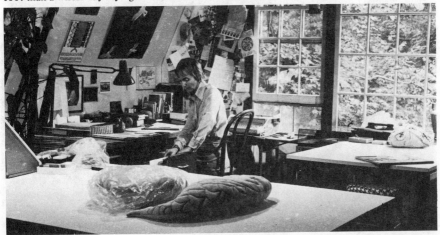

Elsa Brown (Photographer: Jeff Brown)

8.
Coping With Deadlines

"I watch where I am in life and see if I am accomplishing what I want so when I reach the age of death I will not regret things I said I was going to do."

Helen Bitar (Photographer: Jerry Hart)

I operate best with a deadline. I get totally absorbed and intense. (Doris Hoover)

I think deadlines are easier to cope with than the everyday stuff. (Joyce Gross)

When I have a deadline, I get super charged-up and nervous. But I love it. That's when I really implement my tunnel-vision approach to my activity. I put the brakes on a lot of fringe activities, get Kentucky Fried Chicken for the family for supper, and pretty much let the house go (it'll wait, after all!). And what a great feeling of exhilaration when the deadline's met. . . . it's like a heavy weight has been taken off your back and you just might float away. (Lynda Lanker)

Stay up all night to finish it—or delay it for just one more day, except for TV which won't wait and is a killer. (Erica Wilson)

I get more accomplished when I have a deadline . . . I'm very goal oriented. If I don't have one I will establish one. (Joan Michaels-Paque)

"How come you are up so early, Mom?" "I'm not up early—I haven't gone to bed yet." (Fiber artist with a deadline, and child)

●

Deadlines are *pressure*. Most things heat up under pressure, so whether the heat causes flareups within the family or merely fires up your work is largely a matter of individual reaction or response.

Some artists work efficiently and creatively under pressure. Others tend to disintegrate. It is most important to recognize how you respond to deadlines and then *try* to plan accordingly.

I need deadlines. Without them I'd be carried away with all the possibilities and variations and nuances, and would rarely finish the things I started out to do. (If I hadn't had a deadline to make me realistic, I'd still be developing ideas for my first book.)

A deadline often means compromise—with two additional weeks you could polish up your work for a show, could add some of the details that you didn't realize were going to be needed. Yet, knowing when a piece of work is finished is sometimes difficult, and a deadline provides a good stopping point.

Fiber artists meet deadlines with varying degrees of excitement or panic. For some, time-pressure causes apprehension, anxiety and alarm, and these take form in a remarkable variety of physical responses. A few women find themselves obsessed with a need to dust, clean closets, or run errands—anything to avoid facing the deadline! Others get headaches, the trembles, diarrhea, and similar symptoms of stage fright. Barbara Threefoot says: "I panic, get indigestion, and vow not to put myself in the position of having another deadline—everytime." B. J. Adams usually gets "a headache. Deadlines are fine when the unexpected doesn't happen (like relatives dropping in or a business dinner must be planned)." To Sally K. Davidson, "Deadlines usually mean panic," and Rose Dwight adds, "Deadlines kill me! I just work around the clock and we eat at McDonald's much to the delight of my kids."

Other fiber artists thrive on deadlines, enjoying the tension and stimulation. The activity itself seems to generate further energy. Without deadlines, many women find that it's easy to let time drift by or to fritter away energies. Ethel Jane Beitler finds she can

work best when working against a deadline. My brain seems to be more active and I work faster. I dawdle too much when I don't have a deadline. I recall one commission that a fellow artist and I worked on together. I taught during the day, then my co-artist and I met at 3 p.m. and worked until 7, then took a break to eat. Then we'd go back to work again until midnight or later. This regimen kept up for three months, except for one night off a week. My husband must have loved me or the money a great deal to make no complaints.

Deadlines, for many designers and artists, seem to be crucial to the execution and completion of their work. It forces productivity and concentrates energy. Carol Cheney Rome states:

I have to set deadlines to get things done. An inveterate procrastinator, having to do with a rotten self-image, I let a lot of time pass while sweating a new project, squandering the time in anxiety. I work late at night when it's down to the wire.

Kathy Vidak agrees, "I manage because of deadlines! I can really pour the work on when I am forced to. It's not nearly as much fun as the dilly-dallying but things do get done faster with a deadline."

Cam Smith Solari finds that deadlines have a very positive effect on her work.

Deadlines are quite exciting because I always rediscover how much I can get done when I have to. When I have some wild deadline I communicate to my husband about it and get his agreement that it is important and will have priority. I ask his help, drop everything else, and work flat out to meet the deadline. It is amazing what other things you really don't have to do, and how you can just drop everything else for a while and nothing bad happens. Sometimes I use money earned from projects to get food sent in or take us out to dinner.

Deadlines are a simple fact of life in shows, craft sales, exhibitions, design commissions, magazine work or writing. No one enjoys deadline panic, indigestion or headache—yet many of us need the structure or framework of a due date to complete our work. If you accept a design job with a deadline, you must gear up to accomplish it; if you can't, don't accept the work, however much you'd like to do it.

Learning to select time commitments is difficult. Even though I try very hard to avoid deadlines and to keep some time to work for myself, I find this extremely difficult.

Determining what deadlines you are *willing* to accept is certainly a crucial first step, since most fiber artists are conscientious in meeting them. One craftswoman said, regarding her scrupulous regard for due-dates, "I *always* meet my deadlines. It is not a matter of choice." Beatrice Sheftel, adds, "If I promise to do something, I'll keep my work and finish it. Top priority." Nancy Papa says that when she has commitments and deadlines, "The work to be done becomes my time priority and the family manages well (on a temporary basis) without my direction and aid. Sometimes I hate having them find out how little they really need me."

Some women are well organized, efficient, and seem not to get caught short. Deadlines are less of a problem for them. Dona Meilach, author and artist, finds she has

no problems keeping deadlines. Set up realistic deadlines, apportion your time and meet them. If you're not reliable in this business, you cannot be in the business. Realistic deadlines and logical use of time... not waiting until the last minute to accomplish things, will prevent you from being frazzled. Often, I finish things before a deadline and just let them sit until it's time to mail off, exhibit, or whatever.

Sally K. Davidson manages similarly well:

I start a project as soon as I know what's needed and work on it for a time, back off for a while, and then go back and finish it. Generally I get it done before it's due. Most things I do are for books and the author's deadlines have a bit of give.

Ellen Phillips also plans ahead, but has learned to do this only after dealing with difficult pressures:

So far I have managed to push deadlines far enough ahead that they haven't thrown me for too much of a loop. Being organized and a do-ahead person, I get right to work and try not to get caught short. There still are pressures of course. One Christmas—when everything under the sun seemed to have descended on me—I stood at the kitchen sink unable to make up my mind what to do first. The kids were at me and hubby was yelling for dinner. I wondered then if that was what a nervous breakdown felt like. I got through that evening and resolved not to let anything like that happen again. So far it hasn't.

Whether you respond positively or negatively, once you have accepted a deadline, you must face it. Setting the specific date for the completion of a work is the next step. Since craftsmen tend to underestimate the amount of time a work will require, deadlines become the high-tension wires that crisscross our calendars. Even when you make realistic estimates, then double the time, all the available time is consumed in the race to meet the due date. Experience will help, but even after years of work it is not easy to assess the actual time needed. Since no two jobs are identical, there is never an exact parallel to go by.

Always resist being talked into a due date that seems too close. This may be difficult since some commissions rest upon the possibility of completion by a certain date. The installation of art work in a newly constructed building is usually required before the opening. The mayor's ribbon-cutting ceremony is not going to be cancelled for you. Craft fairs, sales, and exhibitions begin on schedule whether or not you are ready. Magazine deadlines are relatively inflexible (a week of leeway may be available at most) because the magazine editors have props to make, rooms to set up, and the schedules of photographers and art directors to meet. Book publishing deadlines are more flexible in practice, though publishers too have schedules involving the coordination of editors, printers, and binders. In the writing of craft books, meeting the deadline is a complex problem because numerous aspects of the work must be pursued simultaneously. Certain examples may be available to be photographed at a time when writing is not yet underway and the exact requirements for individual photographs are still unclear.

Much correspondence is involved in writing a book, particularly if you are using the work of other artists. Packing, shipping, writing, photographing, printing, identifying are all time consuming. It is helpful in a project of this scale to have a series of deadlines. If possible, schedule all the work in blocks, allowing at least an extra month at the end for last minute details.

One of the common deadlines which fiber artists encounter is that for commissioned work. Sometimes the deadline is imposed by a client, or by a publication date. In other cases, you will be asked to state the earliest possible time by which you could have the work completed. To propose such a due date, first carefully estimate how much actual working time will be required. If you need sixty days to complete a piece, be sure you have sixty days *after* your client gives final approval to your sketch or model and you receive a payment (usually twenty-five percent of the agreed-upon price). If you do not specify this, you may find it takes six weeks to get final approval and another two weeks before payment actually arrives. This would leave you with four days in which to do two months worth of work.

If work is to be shipped, does that come out of your allotted time, or is it in addition? Be sure to make it clear to any client how much *working time* you need.

If your work is to be installed in a new building, check periodically to see how the job is progressing. I have worked incessantly, day and night, to finish a commission by the appointed time only to find (as I reached the deadline, bleary-eyed but finished) that the wall on which the work was to be hung had not yet even been plastered.

Try to allow time for the unpredictable—the sprained ankle or the spilled cup of coffee. Once I took some panels outdoors to take progress photos for an interior designer. Then I ran off to the post office and the printer's and came back to find it had rained. One panel had shrunk badly, and it took a prestidigitator's skill to make the changes unnoticeable. It was too late to start over.

Few artists will encounter more interruptions than the homemaker. Just when you count most on your husband to fix dinner and take the kids out to buy new winter jackets, he'll have to go out of town on business. The IRS will decide to audit you on the same day that the washing machine runs over and the architect calls to say they are ready to install your banners. These rear-end collisions of deadlines and duties require hard work and patience from you and from family members. Families learn to cope, and housekeeping gets nicely ignored for a time. Momo Nogano states, "I announce to the family that I am not food shopping, cooking, cleaning, etc. for the next week or whatever the period of extreme pressure is." Robbie Fanning adds, "I go crazy in the head and meet the deadline. Fuck the housework." Gayle Feller says:

I work like hell, staying up all night if necessary. My family can tell by my faraway look that I'm not with them for a few days and they function very nicely without me. Only my body is with them. They cook, I eat without knowing what it is, and go on working.

Elsa Brown describes how she meets her deadlines:

I work like crazy day and night if necessary. When I was working on my book and my dead-line was speeding toward me, I would often be at my typewriter at 5 a.m. The family has to "fudge it" for the required weeks or months and take on more responsibility than usual. If I had the means I would either go away for the necessary period of time or hire help to free me.

Yvonne Porcella squeezes deadlines into her roles of mother, nurse, weaver, designer, and teacher.

If the deadline is short and I really have to push, everything stops while I complete the project. The house doesn't get cleaned, we eat out of cans, children do their own wash. I even some-times give up my day at the hospital as a surgical nurse if I am really pushed for time. I use my day at the hospital as a day of rest because I do not think about deadlines, problems at home, or new designs.

I find that an extra two weeks for emergencies is crucial and minimum regardless of the scale of the work. You can always promise to *try* to have work completed earlier—but don't put yourself into a bind before you begin your work.

Above all, don't schedule projects too close together. There is nothing more ex-hausting than being late on one deadline only to find that when you have finally delivered, another deadline is already pressing.

While I admit to enjoying the challenge and excitement of deadlines, I also re-quire some spaces between to catch up, relax, and get a perspective on my work. It's very important, once a deadline has been met, to share the release from it with the family. Do something special, or frivolous. And do all those things you prom-ised to do as soon as the job was done. Barbara Murdock discusses the importance of this sharing:

When I finish a deadline and collapse, we usually celebrate as a family by going out to dinner. (Mainly because there is nothing edible in the house—as I have not shopped for days.) And I make fervent promises that next time I will (a) say "No," or (b) start earlier. But they know and I know that I won't—it's my way of life.

Jerrie Peters says "no to everything" when she has a job due, but "meeting the deadline is followed up by a great cleanout and virtuous effort to do all those things I promised that I would do after the deadline was over."

Beth Gutcheon adds:

When it is all over, I write the letters that have been waiting for weeks and I call back all the people I have not been dealing with, and apologize very sweetly and explain that I have been mentally ill. I always make the deadline.

Sometimes things go smoothly with a deadline. There is a flow and rhythm and intensity to work which I enjoy. And there is usually enough variety in the de-mands so that I can select work according to how I feel on a particular day. When I can, I sit down and work through my writing, which requires a lot of concentration on my part. If I'm feeling at odds, I can put the studio back in order. If I'm really eager to work with fabrics, I indulge myself and start a new project which I may need as part of the same deadline. If I have to do maintenance-type errands (gro-ceries or pick up kids or whatever) I try to do at least one business-related errand, even if it's just buying a typewriter ribbon or stopping at the fabric shop. Then I still have some sense of accomplishment, and I'm still working towards the deadline.

Sometimes, on the other hand, everything takes longer than I had anticipated, and the deadline looms threateningly close. When it looks hopeless, I get edgy, irritable, and unfair. My family leaves me alone. Someone may bring me a cup of coffee, but usually doesn't speak or stay. I find it easy to apologize for my irascible behavior and it's pretty well understood that I'll probably be that way until the work is finished. I get impatient and upset with myself, for allowing the situation to develop. I vow, openly and loudly, never to let it happen again.

Creative energy cannot always be scheduled in accordance with deadlines and free time. Some days, in the midst of driving or doing errands, or while waiting for your overdue Pap smear report, ideas simply pour forth. You invent and fabricate in a seemingly endless flow and can't *wait* to get back to your work. At other times, when your kids have been invited to spend the day at a friend's and your husband won't be home for dinner, you find a perfect time to work towards your deadline— and your mind goes blank. Bev Rush comments on this phenomenon in her work: "I find it a handicap that in me, being creative is cyclical. At times I just can't click, even though I have time, while other times everything falls into place smoothly and quickly."

I find that every design job has some exciting, creative aspects along with the more mundane elements. If I'm not really clicking, I'll do the measuring, sorting, cutting, or organizing. Sometimes that fires creative energies. And if not, it's always an accomplishment to have finished some part of the work that leads towards making a deadline.

It is also helpful to set smaller goals within the framework of the overall deadline. A daily or a weekly goal can be achieved, whereas the total project sometimes seems endless, a more remote goal. I also reserve some of the best parts of the work as "rewards." If I finish the rewriting of a certain chapter, then I get to hand-sew for the rest of the day. Or if I write twelve letters, then I get to work on new designs. This provides the good feeling of meeting smaller deadlines, along with the pleasure of some of the more delightful aspects of one's work.

Much fiber work can be done in small scraps of time, but some stages of work require solid stretches of concentration. Writing can't be picked up and dropped as readily as quilting, and if you're in the middle of doing an ink drawing, any interruption can spoil the work.

The pressure of deadlines increases the need to "get away" from distractions and disruptions. Even with my children grown and an exceptionally helpful and willing husband at home, uninterrupted hours are rare. I often make use of a few days away from home to resolve last-minute pressure. (It is easy, with writing, to work in a different place. It is not necessarily possible with larger fiber projects: the studio may be the only place that accommodates them.) To make my last book deadline, I went to the ocean for five days. My mother was visiting me at the time and she came along. I got up in the morning, went directly to my writing, had a cup of coffee *served* to me, and wrote! After a few hours I'd dress and we'd walk on the beach. Back to writing. My mother fixed lunch for us and then went off to the beach while I worked in the afternoon. We had a leisurely dinner and a game of

Scrabble, then back to writing in the evening. It was glorious to get so much work done, and to have no schedule, no demands on my time. The utter luxury of feeling no responsibility to anything but my work was exhilarating. And I finished.

Joyce Aiken and I have found similar retreats successful when we work together. We drive to her mountain cabin (car loaded with typewriters, drawing materials, papers, and materials) and we *work*. We stagger out of bed in the morning, sit writing in our nighties until we're tired. Then dress and eat, take a walk, and back to work. In three days at her cabin we can organize all our work for a book.

One can also resort to the local library for a haven, as I did with this book. It's a lot cheaper than a motel. Going to a friend's house is also helpful. Your family has access if you are really needed. You can work uninterrupted, you have a sounding board when you need it, and your friend brings you tea and cookies to sustain you. I have even borrowed the apartment of working friends who are away all day. You can't even look at the mail if you are not at home.

If you have small children or babies at home and don't feel free to leave, you might hire someone to relieve you during those last days. Go into your studio and shut the door.

However you do it, find the temporary space you need to aid you with deadlines. Open time is crucial.

In lieu of this (or along with it) talk to your family. A deadline is never an individual affair; it always involves the rest of the family. Enlist their support. If everyone agrees that your deadline gets top priority, then you are free to work on it while other responsibilities shift. Next, someone else's priority may be most crucial, and there'll be a cooperative effort towards that. In fiber artist Jorjanna Lundgren's family:

We discuss who has crucial commitments for the week and then plan. I meet deadlines by sheer physical torture. I work until my muscles ache and you have to be a little bit crazy to do this. I have 58 banners due in two months and I'll make the deadline.

Barbara Murdock adds:

I procrastinate until the last possible minute and then I work days and hours to get everything done. The house is knee deep in my clutter. The kids and Jim clean house, go for hamburgers or pizza while I am involved in these marathon productions. I become cranky, irritable, haggard, unkempt—cursing anyone and everything involved. I generally finish (often with only minutes to spare—at the most a few hours). We call this "Racing with TIME"—my only worry is that with age I may be getting too old to run the race.

Deadlines will always be part of a professional life in fibers. The degree of pressure exerted by the deadline depends upon the intensity of your commitment and your particular arrangement.

Perhaps the most important element in handling deadlines is understanding your own responses and reactions to them. If they fire you to action, as they do most fiber artists, you can accept them. If pressure makes you fall apart avoid all deadlines. But to simplify the handling of deadlines, when they are unavoidable, always keep these factors in mind: (1) allow yourself ample time to complete the work, (2) add extra time for emergencies and miscalculations, (3) check periodically with the client on the progress of the total job, (4) enlist the understanding, support, and assistance of your family, (5) hire outside help as you need to or can afford it, (6) allow yourself some uninterrupted time to meet the final deadline, (7) concentrate, finish the work, and (8) relax and celebrate the completion with your family.

If you follow this advice, with each deadline you meet you'll be better able to re-evaluate your time allotment for the entire process and know better how to handle the next similar situation. Each time a due date arrives you can look back and see how you managed, where things went well or wrong, what you failed to allow for. And you can look at your work and realize that you *finished*—from concept to completed, actual work. Once the statement is made, there is a really good feeling of achievement and, one hopes, of having excelled. You have executed another piece of work to view, to evaluate and to consider in terms of your own progress or growth as an artist.

When I have a deadline, there are several things I do:
  . . . bitch a lot
  . . . use more convenience foods
  . . . try to get all the laundry done so at least things are in clean *heaps in the basement*
  . . . know that things will ease up and after it's all over I can put the house and my head back in shape
  . . . work until 1 or 1:30 a.m.
  . . . vow never to get myself in that position again!
(Sharon Lappin Lumsden)

I try to plan ahead and work like hell to meet deadlines. If I don't have the projects done—I put in something else. Unfortunately most of my work is too gross for public understanding or buying so I have 300 art pieces at home to choose from. (Madge Copeland)

When I have a deadline as I do for my columns or commission work I steal time from one or another duty to accomplish my deadline. But I do not steal time from just one area. I steal a little here and a little there or give up a Sunday outing or hire a helper for three days. Deadlines are only what you want to make of them. (Bucky King, threadbender and fiber artist from Wyoming)

Without deadlines I would be a bum and lie in the sun all day. I like the discipline of a deadline and usually manage to finish a project a few minutes before the guillotine falls. My family cooperates completely during these crises, often eating out a lot and speaking little. (Joyce Aiken)

Deadlines keep me going and producing and always will. Without deadlines I would not get anything done.
  As most of my professional work is done for the magazines, deadlines are not funny. But my assignments are always in before the deadline. If I do not have a magazine deadline, or a deadline for a show, then I set up my own deadlines. . . . "I will have this, this, and this done before September 1st or before my company arrives." I need and enjoy deadlines. (Carole Austin)

A deadline spurs me on (it is an outside stimulus) and somewhere I get the efficiency and willpower to meet it. I've stayed up all night, I've worked right through mealtimes, etc. Fortunately my family is flexible and often will pitch in, etc. Deadlines are mainly devices to keep me going! (Gini Hill)

With deadlines, something has to give! Usually I postpone such things as vacuuming, dusting, cleaning silver, etc. . . . We entertain a lot so some of my deadlines conflict. . . . (Lari Ehni, fiber artist, mother of seven)

I work like a dog night and day. Sometimes when I'm really pushed, the children are taken off for a day by their father or by my parents—like on a Saturday or a Sunday and I can get a lot of work done with no meals to fix, no baths to run, etc. (Karen Jahncke)

"I have never tried or claimed to be a good housekeeper. My work has priority. When it goes well, I go well and I am then a good person to live with."

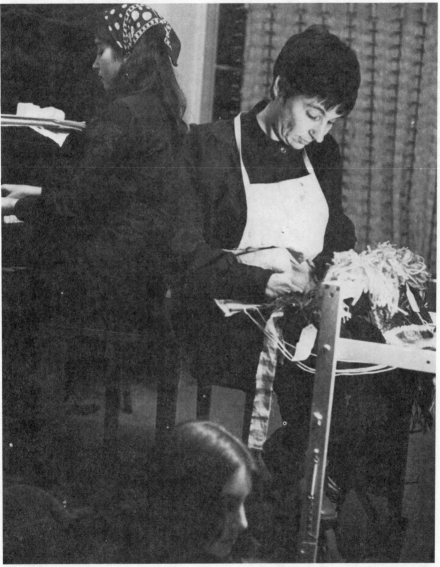

Shirley Fink (Photographer: Stan Fink)

9.
Supporting Yourself

"I knew before I was married what I needed to feel whole and with what intensity I would pursue it. I frequently make priority lists. Also, to be honest, I expect a great deal from my family but not more than I am willing to do myself."

Joan Michaels-Paque (Photographer: Henry P. Paque)

Can I support myself? Yes. Yes. Yes. I like carrying my own weight. It has much to do with my identity as an artist. While the girls were small I wanted to be financially supported because I felt I was doing an important job. (Joan Michaels-Paque)

I support myself as an artist, meaning I can pay for the studio, my materials, and related education and travel, but I'm a "kept woman" as far as room and board. Inside, I'm angry about my inability to support my whole person, first with myself that my work ethic requires this of me as part of my self-respect (a personal problem that is possible to change) and with society that it does not value the textile art object to the same degree it will support other media (a social problem that is possible to change but I may have arthritis by then). (Nancy Papa)

No, I cannot support myself. I find this very depressing. I teach workshops, exhibit my work, sell it in shops, etc. I will never be able to produce enough work to support myself. (Elizabeth Fuller)

I do support myself through my work in direct and indirect ways but always wondering when I shall have to go out and get a job that is not related to my work. (Helen Bitar)

•

Once you have "found" the time and the space for your work and have resolved some of the problems of family and home, you can also consider the possibility of earning an income in your field. Although few fiber artists support themselves solely through the design and production of art objects, selling your art can provide a good supplemental source of income.

While I'm sure there must be some fiber artists who limit their work to a single area, I personally don't know any. It is almost a necessity, if one is to earn a living through fibers, to have a broader range of activities. Beth Gutcheon, for instance, says:

I do support myself but not Jeffrey and we split the expenses of David. And I do not believe I could make a living making quilts which is one of the things I love best. I can do pretty well teaching, lecturing and writing about quilts. But actually at least half of my income at this point comes from other kinds of writing . . . usually about crafts, but not always.

Constance Howard, artist and author of several books agrees: "I could not support myself, not without teaching. I have always taught."

Many women *believe* they could support themselves entirely through their art work even though they are not doing so. Either it has not been necessary, or they are teaching or employed in related jobs. Most women feel they could not support themselves *and* their families without making some adjustments in their life- or work-styles, and they are not enthusiastic about that prospect. Says Peggy Moulton:

I could support myself if I could find a way to get along without eating. I thoroughly enjoy what I am doing and do it only to please myself. Therefore, my work doesn't appeal to a lot of people. Plus the fact that I'm not going to give my stuff away so my prices are high. In a real emergency I could (or would) change my tactics so that I could find a wider market without compromising my aesthetics.

Sharon Lappin Lumsden states:

I suspect I could support myself with weaving but I would have to make some changes: (1) apply for food stamps, and (2) develop more "production" items and a steady wholesale market.

But I'm not sure I would try to support myself on the weaving, because of the negative compromises that might be required . . . .

Similarly, Shirley Fink says she

could support myself through my work if I wished to change my design orientation. That is, if I chose to do either production work or limit myself to two-dimensional tapestries . . . . I do neither of these. I supply an income from teaching in my field.

And Gayle M. Feller sums it up, "What I do know is that I do not want to become a manufacturing machine."

Various fabric artists have pursued their interests single-mindedly, and managed to make it pay. It *is* possible to create your own job—determine the kind of work you'd like most to do and then do just that. It takes a lot of drive and energy; so does creating your own job in most other fields.

Some women find it essential to their self-respect to be able to support themselves. They enjoy the self-esteem and independence that come with being self-sufficient. Income from one's work provides a kind of freedom—not just financial independence, but an expanded range of choices.

Many craftswomen have commented on the satisfactions of carrying their own weight financially. They do not want their husbands or partners to have to feel responsible for them: it seems a heavy burden for men to always carry alone. However, when one's children are small, a mother needs financial (and every other kind of) support she can get. As Rivkah Sweedler says, "I need money for fibers. But . . . I'm physically very dependent, having four children. . . . I could go out and work as a therapist again and make money but that's denying the need I have to work for myself."

One of the most satisfying sources of income is through selling one's art work, but it is usually necessary to find additional means of income to be self-supporting. Among the possibilities—all discussed later in this chapter—are teaching, lecturing, doing architectural and interior commissions, designing, and writing. In order for any of these to be successfully pursued, the artist and her work must have considerable public exposure.

Exposure

The continuous exposure of your work is crucial. If one artist is well known and another is unheard of, the difference does not necessarily lie in artistic merit. One may just be a better and more visible promoter than the other.

The most direct way to show work is through exhibitions, whether in co-ops, galleries, banks, lobbies, or showrooms. The important thing is to get your work out where it can be seen. There is no assurance it will be purchased from a show, but it most certainly isn't going to be sold from your closet.

Unless your talents are exceptionally rare, gallery directors will not beat a path to your door panting and pounding loudly for the privilege of buying your work. You have to *look* for exhibitions. And don't be too snobbish about where you will show. Surprises pop up in unexpected places. Any seed planted may sprout like Jack's magic bean stalk.

Years ago, I showed my first stitchery pieces to a friend who worked for the American Crayon Company in Los Angeles. She asked to show my work in the sales area open to teachers. I agreed, though a few of my friends felt I should hold out for a museum or gallery show. Subsequently, American Crayon asked if they could send the work on to their New York showroom. Of course I said they could, knocking over chairs in my dash to report the good news to friends. The New York office was in Rockefeller Plaza, where the show was seen by a staff member from the Contemporary Crafts Museum, who invited me to exhibit there. A New York show! I was lucky, but it was due to some unpretentious initial exposure.

On another occasion I entered a quilt in the Eastern States Quilt Exposition. It was my first quilt, a contemporary appliqué. A few of my (non-exhibiting) painting friends considered the exhibition low in status. I didn't win any prizes, but I did hear from one of the jurors. That was Roxa Wright, who has contributed so much to the needle arts in America, who was then an editor at *House Beautiful* magazine. She came to Stanford to see me and commissioned my first article. That article led to free-lance designing and directed my energies to writing.

My experiences suggest that *all* exposure is valuable. How can you be "discovered" if your work is not visible? An exhibit at the Metropolitan Museum of Art in New York might be your idea of the "best," but I wouldn't suggest you hide your work under the proverbial bushel while you wait for an invitation to show there. Go ahead and exhibit in the lobby of the local savings and loan.

Because my fiber work has had good exposure, I have found no shortage of jobs. Fortunately, I have never yet clutched my portfolio in clammy hands and approached an architect or design firm, nor have I sought out a teaching or lecturing position. Perhaps *now* I could call on an architect without trepidation, but there was a time when I'd have been too frightened by the prospect. (Where were women's assertiveness classes when *I* needed them?)

My contacts came primarily through exhibitions and later from installed work. Magazines usually contact me, though a few times I have submitted projects to them by mail, which is less intimidating than a personal confrontation. I am fairly brave facing my typewriter. I assume that if I actually *pursued* possible clients and commissions, I would have more work than I could handle.

With adequate exposure it *is* possible to support yourself, or at least the possibility is becoming more credible all the time. Public awareness and acceptance of fiber arts is increasing. But the number of women producing fiber art is also increasing, so the competition is keener. You must know what you want to do. Don't approach selling initially in terms of the market, of what will sell, or what will pay. Decide first what you most want to devote yourself to. It is, after all, the hours of your life with which you are bartering.

"It takes a certain amount of courage to begin a new career at age 60 . . . After 20 years of snatching bits of time, to do the thing I loved best—working with my hands—I feel that I made the right decision."

De Loris Stude (Photographer: Wendell Stude)

"I know of so many young craftsmen who turn out an astounding amount of work with children underfoot and a skeptical husband in the TV room. If you know what you want to do and work hard at it, the whole thing seems not so difficult to sort out."

Florence Pettit (Photographer: Thomas F. Ryan)

Being Professional

To earn a living as a fiber artist requires dedication. It also requires persistence, courage, and some rigidity of the upper lip. It is not easy to approach a potential client or a gallery with photos and sketches that represent the sum total of your life's work in your hand and a lump in your throat and know that a response of complete indifference is a distinct possibility. Or worse: to discover that they think your work is really awful.

Being professional is largely a matter of attitude towards oneself and one's work. It requires, as Carole Austin puts it,

exposure and lots of hard work. . . . It is that one is serious and devoted to what she does. It is not just a free-time hobby. And it is a continuous thing with long-term goals. Coupled with this, one must be able to be critical about her work. You have to know exactly where your work stands. Does it meet the required standards to be sold in a store or bought by a magazine? So many women try these things time and again and are so discouraged because they never make a go of it. It makes me so angry because they approach it from a housewife's rather than a professional's point of view, and it is so hard to get it across to them. When I speak to my students about this I always use the Olympics as an example. Those athletes don't simply go out one day and try out for the team . . . they begin at a very early age working hours upon hours. The arts are no different. You get to be a superstar by lots and lots of grueling hard work. You learn darn early that no one is going to come knocking at your door no matter how good you are (unless you are superstar status). You have got to work and keep your name and your art before the public, and you have got to sell your work.

You must learn to be professional. That doesn't mean you have to conform to any stereotype—it only means doing your best work and presenting it attractively, being objective about it, and being able to handle all aspects of it, including business and public relations.

Business cards and letterhead stationery are helpful in establishing a professional status. Obviously, you can survive without them, but they offer a quick visual identity and ensure that your phone number and mailing address are readily available. They often have a positive effect on your own attitude towards your work as they represent a commitment to it. A logo, a personal trademark, or a distinctive signature all serve to identify (and therefore advertise) your work.

Resumé

Part of your professional equipment includes a written resumé, which lists your qualifications—education, experience, and so on. The content of a resumé may vary according to the particular job or assignment for which you are applying.

Keep a complete resumé in your own files. Include dates and locations of all exhibits, group shows, commissions, teaching jobs, degrees, courses, workshops, awards, etc. From this, draw the pertinent information for a brief resumé when you need it. A well-written half page is more likely to be read than three solidly filled pages. Type the information neatly on your letterhead, or add your name, phone, and address to each sheet. A standard resumé may include any of the following: biography, education, degrees, special training, professional organizations, work experience, commissions, publications, lectures, consulting, honors and awards. But be selective.

If you feel limited in some areas of the resumé, be sure to consider work which you may have volunteered or energies expended through organizations. For example, if you handled the publicity and promotion for a fund-raising, or designed advertising for a faculty scholarship fund drive, include it. Work for civic organizations is valuable experience, even though it was not salaried. The resumé lays out your areas of expertise. Simply omit any areas where you feel a lack.

Presenting Your Work. Any presentation or portfolio must be well thought out and carefully displayed. It should include your resumé.

In making contact to show your work remember that all businesses, whether their specific function is directed towards sales, community cultural enrichment, or education purposes, prefer to receive a letter of inquiry first. Then arrange an appointment so that you can bring in actual work and a portfolio. Find out, if possible, how much time you will be given, so that you can plan accordingly.

A portfolio usually consists only of two-dimensional work—photographs, drawings, plans or sketches of your work and commissions. A presentation can consist of models, slides, photographs, or actual pieces. Always put your name on your slides or photographs. Once they are separated from your portfolio (or letter), only you would know they were yours. Add your name, address, and phone number to each item—photo, clipping, slide, sample—that you submit.

Have a neat and attractive portfolio cover or container for your work. Entering an office balancing papers and boxes stacked eye-high gives a poor impression. Show only your best and have at hand all the pertinent information—size, price, weight, method of installation, etc. The material should be organized so that nobody's time is wasted while you turn slides right-side-up, reassemble your model, or search your notes for a list of materials. Include related material you consider significant in your work, such as magazine articles, newspaper clippings, and announcements of exhibits. The portfolio should be well organized, with all materials mounted neatly.

Be sure to leave a business card or note that clearly states your name, address, and phone number. A brochure, folder, or even a single good photograph with this information attached will serve as a visual reminder of your work. A brief resume is helpful. Avoid excessively long lists of shows and commissions—a few good ones will more likely be read.

Pricing Your Work. A professional *expects* to be paid for her work and should never let anyone assume it is free. If you wish to donate work, of course, you still can. But do not deprecate yourself or your work by giving it away as a matter of course. Too often women's work is considered a pasttime, something you just do in your free time. "The clue is to take what you do seriously, think of it as work and believe you *deserve* the time and energy it takes to do it," says Ann Syer. "If you refer to it as your hobby, something to 'keep you busy,' then all is lost."

Unless you regard yourself as a professional and act accordingly, others will not treat you as one. Having your name gold-leafed on the office door is not a prerequisite of professionalism; self-esteem is.

Even though few artists consider payment either the motivation or the real reward for their work, they recognize that it is significant, and it is one accepted measure of your work's importance.

Each year at least twelve organizations (hospital, symphony, museum) as well as church, alumni, and charity groups ask me to donate a piece of work for auction or sale. Good exposure? Sure. But don't assume an obligation, and contribute more than you want to. Don't feel guilty if you say "No," even when your friends donate their time to the worthy organizations that solicit your contribution. You get exposure, yes, but it can be costly advertising. I enjoy participating and helping *locally* within reasonable limits, but now I decide in advance each year what I will give away. Then I (graciously) decline all other requests on the basis that I have already selected my donations for the year.

Even though I approach my work professionally in most ways, I continue to dislike discussing money. I now handle financial negotiations by letter rather than discussing it directly, because I feel comfortable that way. Find out what works best for you. I have finally learned not to commit myself to anything on the telephone. This way I avoid giving a spur of the moment "Yes," or making an impulsive decision which (if I gave it five minutes of contemplation) I would flatly say "No" to. Letters also provide a record of what has been offered and agreed upon.

Putting a price on one's work is one of the most difficult aspects of selling it. There is often a discrepancy between the effort and time invested and a workable selling price, or between personal value and market value.

You must first decide whether or not a piece really is for sale. Barbara Murdock doesn't like parting with her quilts: "I can honestly say that I really am not anxious to sell work—but I do like to show it. I have sold some things and then almost instantly regretted it! It's almost like selling your children!"

Don't sell a piece if you are not ready to part with it. To overprice a work because you want to keep it may make all of your prices suspect. It is better just to mark the piece NFS (Not For Sale) until you're ready to sell it. You will find that the more work you do, the less possessive about it you become. If you find that you'd sell anything the minute someone asks, try giving your work away to someone in the family.

In pricing, experience is a helpful teacher. As you learn to value your time and energy and talent, you will find it less difficult to put a monetary value on your own work.

If you find yourself reluctant to discuss prices, and you sell direct, make it easier on yourself by writing down the prices of all your works for sale. And don't do it at the last minute. Make out a price list and then let it settle. A week later you will wonder how you thought a particular piece of cloth was worth $40, or why you were giving away another piece for just $80.

A prepared list avoids any faltering, mixup, or misunderstanding (someone sends you a check for $15 when you know you said $50). And it also helps keep you from changing your mind or making spur-of-the-moment decisions when you have a client in front of you.

The value of a work is not necessarily related to time, though this is often a consideration. Its value has little to do with the materials used, either, but material costs may enter into pricing as well. Various fiber artists have arrived at systems or methods of pricing which work for them, and some may work for you. Following are a few guidelines that may be helpful. These refer primarily to the sales of art work, not to fees for design or teaching, which are discussed later in this chapter.

Pricing according to function may seem absurd, yet it *is* often a realistic factor. A pillow, for example, rarely commands the same price as a wall hanging of comparable size and complexity. One is considered a usable object and the other "art," at least by the general buying public. Art has an indeterminate value, whereas a functional object can be compared with other similar objects. This explains why hand-sewn pillows typically fall into a close price range. The average pillow sells for about $20, although some may go for as little as $8 or as much as $60. A panel of the same size, made into a wall hanging, may sell for considerably more—if it sells. The pillow *does* have the appeal of a functional object and may be more likely to sell just because of that.

Many buyers are afraid to make aesthetic judgments, or to respond personally to art work. When they buy a pillow, there is no need to justify or defend the purchase: they have bought a pillow. When they buy a wall hanging, they have made an aesthetic choice. They often feel on less safe ground. So if you're producing a functional object you will probably want to consider the going price of similar pieces. To the artist who has just finished a six-inch square of the world's most beautiful embroidery, the handwork speaks for itself. In an art gallery it may be viewed as an exquisite, small tapestry. But if it is sewn to a pillow or shirt, the buyer does not consider it art. He is buying a pillow or a shirt.

Pricing by the square foot may also sound absurd, but I have found it an excellent way to set prices, especially on large-scale two-dimensional work. Architects tend to think in terms of square-foot costs on all other materials that are installed—tile, carpeting, cork, wood—and since commissioned art work for interior use is sometimes considered a permanent installation, it tends to be similarly categorized. This system is rarely applied to smaller pieces, which are regarded like paintings. If you are a well-known artist, of course, none of this is likely to apply. It would be indiscreet (at the least) to ask Louise Nevelson a square-foot price for a wall. But many architects and interior designers do not know the name of even one fiber artist, so they'll hardly be purchasing your work on the basis of reputation. Their concern is with enriching walls visually at a price per square foot.

Per-foot pricing information is not difficult to determine, and you may be surprised how satisfactory this method is. Take one large-scale piece you have finished and sold as a starting point. Suppose you did a quilted wall hanging, four by six feet, and sold it for $480. Let's assume that the price seemed satisfactory to you, and, since you did sell it, it was obviously satisfactory to a buyer. So, on that 24-square-foot panel, you received $20 a square foot. If you are asked to do a five-by-eight-foot panel of a similar nature, you now have a guide for pricing. The 40-square-foot panel at $20 a foot would cost $800. The final cost per square foot may be adjusted according to total size, complexity, whether you deliver and install the work, and other details. I usually quote a price related to a specific sketch or model, and then try to suggest a price range going above or below depending on the flexibility of the design. For example, suppose you have determined the cost to be between $25 and $35 a square foot. If your client chooses the lower estimate, you may cut down on hand-sewn details in a stitchery mural, or simplify forms in a wood panel. If the higher estimate is agreed upon, you have a marvelous opportunity to elaborate the complex details that add so much to any work.

This per-square-foot method is an excellent guide for quoting prices on commissions, but it is not necessarily the best way to price individual pieces which have already been finished. When you produce a panel first, and then hope to find a buyer, the situation is different. Now you can make an aesthetic evaluation which may raise or lower the square-foot cost. Also, suppose you have made five panels, two of which sell immediately at your price. The others may stay with you for a couple of years, and as your work and style develop you may no longer feel those are works you wish to sell. So in doing your individual work, you should consider that element of risk, along with the relative freedom you have (you need not work within a color scheme, or a size limitation, etc. as you do in commissions).

Pricing according to time spent on a piece offers a precarious and sometimes tricky guide. How long you work on a piece surely is a consideration, but it's not the answer to pricing. It is possible to devote months to a work that you find doesn't quite come off. If the work is not satisfying to you, in aesthetic or visual terms, then is it worth anything at all? A 30-second sketch done by a great artist like Matisse or Picasso on a linen napkin is worth a lot of money. In these instances there is no direct ratio of price to time.

One approach to pricing by time is to compare your art work to full-time employment. If your salary as a teacher would be $1000 a month (or $250 a week, $50 a day), should you receive about the same for art work? If you are making a soft sculpture in two days, you might price it at $100.

Unfortunately, much craft work is extraordinarily time-consuming. Jo Morris points out, "Not all fiber artists find self-support a possibility. It is difficult for me to get what I feel is a decent price for the designing and work I put into a piece. Hand stitching takes so long—and as a potter remarked to me, 'Most women can sew.'"

Thus, each person must weigh her decision regarding the appropriateness of pricing when time involvement is great. Craft work is too often sold at a price which undervalues the craftsman's time, but sometimes that is the only way it will sell. If you spend 200 hours making a quilt, and calculate that your time is worth $5 an hour, you would put a $1,000 price tag on your work, and this might eliminate the possibility of sale. If someone offers you $60, that's about 30 cents an hour, and it doesn't take the cost of materials or overhead into account.

Remember that you have to consider *all* your costs, including materials and the expense of running a business, as well as your time. If you buy $5 worth of materials and make ten small dolls, your materials cost a mere 50 cents per doll. A weaving may use $60 worth of yarns. If you rent a studio or just use electricity at home, write business letters, advertise, these expenses contribute to your overhead. Add up your monthly expenses, and apportion them among the pieces you make. If you make ten pieces a month, the price of each should include about one tenth of that month's expenses, assuming all ten pieces are sold. The difficulty of covering all such costs by what is actually sold accounts for the presence of so many fiber artists in home studios, where overhead does not have to be covered directly by sales.

On the other side of the balance, take into consideration the fact that you are doing precisely what you want, at your own convenience, that you are your own master and have no faculty meetings, parent-teacher conferences or social obligations. You don't have to drive to work, you don't need new clothes to wear to an office, you don't require a full-time baby sitter, you don't eat lunch out. Consider too the number of hours you work per day. Those advantages may make you more willing to accept less for doing your own work. Given all the advantages of working at home, is your income acceptable?

I am sometimes resentful that I'm not as well paid as I would be in comparable jobs within a business or institution, where I would also enjoy vacation or sick leave or health care. But I consciously choose this over other kinds of work. I always hope that I will make the bestsellers' list or that a fabulous commission will drop into my lap so that I can let up for a year. But while I wait for these fantasies to materialize, I work hard, I enjoy my work, and I have a reasonable income from it.

If when all these aspects are considered, a fair price for your time makes your work look like a national treasure, there are still a few alternatives. One is to sell your designs, retaining the original pieces. Another (unless you need the cash) is to trade—to exchange it for other art work or for services. Both of these approaches are discussed later in this chapter. A third consideration is that your work may actually be worth every penny of the high price, and the problem becomes one of gaining the right exposure for it to sell.

Finding the buyer or outlet that will pay your price takes time. It may mean sending photos or slides away to galleries, collectors, or museums who have an interest in your particular field. Many artists feel it is essential to establish the proper value of their work, even though this reduces the number of sales.

Pricing must also be based on where and how your work is sold. An exclusive resort gift shop is patronized by people less concerned with the price tag than those at a church bazaar. Work should be selected accordingly. A crafts fair or street sale eliminates many of the costs of overhead, so of course selling prices can reflect this. If you sell directly, you are spared the cost of commissions, insurance, and paperwork involved in exhibitions or selling in shops and galleries. However, some craftsmen do not want to be involved in selling, or do it only casually. If you sell through a shop, gallery, or other outlet, you must take its commission into consideration when pricing your work.

You should have a clear idea of what you must personally receive for each piece. Then add on the commission. If each item you make is one-of-a-kind, your prices can vary from one to the next. However, if you make comparable items and sell from your own studio as well as a local shop, you must resolve any price discrepancy. A shopowner may reasonably object if a customer can find virtually identical work available at two different prices. Thus, when a shop takes a percentage, you must either raise your own direct-sale price or give the shop owner a discount to maintain identical selling prices. For example, you may produce soft-sculpture figures for a retail price of $25. (That's your selling price to the individual buyer and the selling price used by the shop.) However, when the shop buys from you, it deducts the agreed-upon discount or their "markup." If you allow them a 50 percent discount, then they purchase the pieces from you at $12.50 each. By limiting your sales to either retail or wholesale only, this problem is eliminated.

If you are involved in production work, you'll find good assistance for pricing in various craft magazines and small business manuals. These are often based on a ratio of cost and time per item. It is a more complicated procedure based on somewhat standard production practices which consider overhead, depreciation, maintenance costs, etc. on an annual basis. Look for professional help for this kind of pricing, and seek the aid of professional journals. The U.S. Department of Labor and the Small Business Administration have booklets available free or at nominal cost to help you in determining the organization of a production business. One of your most reliable sources will be other craftsmen who have been involved in the same work, and local or national crafts organizations.

The prices of any individual artist's work will vary to some extent in response to demand. Quilts, for example, have soared in value compared to ten years ago, with antique quilts commanding highest prices. While the per-hour income for handmade quilts still doesn't equal what a plumber makes, it is rising steadily.

The old law of supply and demand is still alive and well (since there are no crafts subsidies to artificially support prices). When everything you do is grabbed up before the last knot is tied or while the dye is still wet, you can readily see that demand exceeds supply and you can price accordingly, charging more.

If you have a lot of work which doesn't move, and you *want* or *need* to sell it, then you may have to recognize that your supply exceeds the demand and lower your prices, or try another market place. The success of your sales gives you an indication of the response to your price range. It does not necessarily have anything to do with value. We are talking about selling, not evaluating the worth of the work.

Pricing according to subjective evaluation of your own work offers a final basis for determining selling price. You can make this evaluation yourself, or you can ask other artists, craftsmen, critics, friends, appraisers, or gallery owners. It is a difficult task and one based on a variety of things including personal response, knowledge of current art scene, the particular city or town in which you live or sell, and other intangibles. A piece which has high artistic value for one area may be disregarded by another. The quilt a folk gallery raves over may be disregarded by an art gallery. A piece the art gallery features may be rejected by the gift shop.

Evaluations according to artistic merit will vary tremendously, but it is important that you arrive at a price which is comfortable to you. Be as objective and critical of your own work as possible—try to respond to your own sense of the work's artistic merit.

In making a pricing judgment about your own work, you may think you have no idea at all where to start. At that point ask your visiting aunt or a neighbor or the postman to name a price. You'll find you can react quite readily to their suggestions, finding them either absurdly high, insultingly low, or perfectly reasonable. Having the suggestion helps because it gives you a starting point.

Trading Work. Almost all artists and craftsmen enjoy the process of marketing their work through exchanges. You are not limited to trading with other artists, though that is easier because your valuation of time is similar. It is helpful to have established prices on the particular works to be traded, thereby offering a basis for the trade. At other times the price may be set on services or on a particular piece and you can produce a work of comparable value.

Some years ago when my son needed dental work, I traded a stitchery mural for the orthodontist's services. My husband has traded sculpture for medical care, for studio cleaning, for electrical work, and for legal assistance.

The feasibility of trading depends to some extent on your reputation or the appeal of your work. The accountant or washing-machine repairman is not likely to be interested in a trade (but never fail to inquire). It is often simply a matter of people helping one another, each doing what he can do best. Some trades amount to a mutual gift-giving: others are business arrangements and must be regarded as such in your records and accounting.

If you are not dependent on your art for the cash income, it's often more satisfactory to give the work away than to undersell it. I've never been able to sell a quilt—I'd be too embarrassed to ask for what I thought one was worth. But I have enjoyed making them for friends or family.

Giving work to friends is probably one of the greatest joys of the hand arts. But it is important that the work be appreciated, since the recipient's enjoyment is your only return on the work (other than the rewards of creating it). I have so often heard stitchers lament that their work is disregarded—a sister-in-law supposes the pillow will be useful, or that the baby quilt (while nice) is not really the "right" blue to go with the bedroom. An aunt asks if the tapestry is "supposed to look like something." Responses like these make you feel you've sent a child off to the orphanage. At least when work is sold you have financial compensation, and the knowledge that someone liked it enough to plunk down hard cash.

I have given work away, somewhat impulsively, to people just because of the way they enjoyed it. That's fun to do, but if income is what you need, then a cash sale has multiple rewards.

Keeping Records. Being a professional also requires you to keep records. It is crucial to keep track of all expenditures and income. Tax laws governing home studios change from year to year. It is important to get advice as early as possible, since it may affect many aspects of the way work is handled. Seek competent advice: a CPA or tax attorney, consulted early, can offer valuable information. Check with your library, other local artists, and organizations such as the American Crafts Council or your craft guild. There are excellent books, pamphlets, and brochures to assist you. Artist's Equity publishes *Taxes and the Artist*, which covers recent changes in the tax codes. *The Visual Artist and the Law* (published by Praeger) includes a discussion of various legal problems as well as the tax problems of the artist. Howard W. Connaughton, C.P.A., has published a book for *Craftsmen in Business: A Guide to Financial Management and Taxes* (American Crafts Council). The Department of the Treasury, Internal Revenue Service, has a free pamphlet entitled *Tax Guide for Small Business*, which covers accounting methods and business deductions.

Another valuable reference is *Career Opportunities in Crafts* (Crown Publishers) by Elyse Sommer, who exemplifies what she advises in her book—that is, the importance of developing versatility. As an author, agent, craftsperson, and lecturer, each of her activities supports the others.

Norbert N. Nelson's *Selling Your Crafts* (Van Nostrand Reinhold) includes good basic information on how to sell profitably what you produce. It covers bookkeeping, copyrighting, tax records, and legal considerations, and lists buying offices, crafts publications, and marketing centers. The American Crafts Council's *Contemporary Craft Market Place* is another aid for craftsmen seeking sales outlets. New guides are being published constantly—check your library.

Get the best professional help you can find and afford. Pool your problems and questions with other craftspeople and if need be seek the assistance of an expert as a group rather than individually.

Where To Sell and Show Your Work. There are many places to sell art work. It may require investigation and sometimes ingenuity to develop them. Among the more obvious sales spots are galleries and exhibitions, retail shops, fairs, direct sales from your studio, and co-op arrangements. And you need not limit yourself strictly to your own locality.

Gallery exhibitions offer a good—and prestigious—opportunity to sell. Read the art papers for your area, find out where and when open or competitive shows are scheduled, take courage, and enter. Only the person who has never tried has never been rejected. Being rejected does not necessarily mean your work is poor. It only means it was unacceptable, or inappropriate, for that particular exhibition. A piece rejected in one show may win a prize in another. A rejection does give you pause to re-evaluate, of course. You should (with all the objectivity you can muster) cast a critical eye on your own work. If you conclude your work is good, enter it again.

More than one woman has found great challenge and even inspiration from rejection and disparaging criticism (many critics long felt that fabrics did not belong in any show). Lee Erlin Snow, artist and author, says "There is a local crafts critic who has inadvertently helped me. By his 'putting me down' I have worked harder to show myself that I can."

Positive encouragement is still, of course, what we need most. For every artist spurred on by rejection there may be several who are utterly defeated by it. I know of one group of stitchery artists who work together periodically. They decided to have a rejection-slip burning, and found they had an ample collection for a dazzling conflagration! Each was surprised to find she was not the only one who had ever been rejected. The upshot of the burning was that they banded together, organized a show of their own, found a gallery, and put on a successful fiber exhibition.

You can gear your work for a particular show, of course. If the exhibit is in the local art museum, your large hangings will fare better than they will at the flea-market crafts show, where lots of small, inexpensive items sell.

One- or two-person gallery shows are obviously the most desirable. Viewers will remember your name and your work, you receive the best press coverage, and the greatest opportunity for recognition through sales.

Write to galleries and ask for an appointment to come in and submit your work. Showing in small exhibitions often leads to invitations for major gallery shows. One-woman shows in bank lobbies, business foyers, and interior design shops are worth doing if you're interested in sales and further exhibitions.

Major museums and civic or university galleries are usually endowed or funded in such a way that exhibitions can be selected without any concern for the saleability of the work. These exhibitions are the "plums." Private galleries must be self-supporting and exhibitions in them are not easy to obtain. Each usually has its own direction in terms of the kinds of work shown. Familiarity with the gallery will help you determine the appropriateness of your work for that gallery.

There are relatively few galleries that devote themselves to fiber arts. The director of one California crafts gallery commented: "I'm having to cut down on fiber and contemporary craft shows. Rent raises, etc. are forcing me to be very realistic about a prospective show's saleability."

Another feels that "there is no indication that private persons are collecting more fiber arts."

And a criticism offered was:

Fiber artists often feel no responsibility toward the care and maintenance feasibility of their work. . . . They often don't provide any practical means of hanging or displaying the work.

If, in spite of the difficulties, you have been accepted for a gallery show, you should clarify the business arrangements. A gallery may take up to a 50-percent commission on sales, but it also provides benefits—a clientele, an opening, a mailing list, a brochure or announcement, a poster, a preview for press and patrons, excellent installation of work, and professional dealings with buyers. A gallery show involves having your work on exhibit in what amounts to a consignment arrangement.

Selling on consignment means placing your work in a shop or exhibition area on a speculative basis. That is, the shop does not purchase the work from you, and only when it is sold to a customer do you get your percentage of the sale. For the beginning craftsman, consignment is often the only way she can get her work shown. Most artists and craftsmen have worked on consignment at some time, especially when getting started. While nobody would prefer it, if you have no other choices it must be considered.

Many fiber artists will not place *any* work on consignment because they feel that shops buy all their merchandise outright except for hand-crafted work. This seems discriminatory, and the unreasonableness is compounded if the commission is high. But if you are very anxious to sell your work, it may be the only avenue open to you.

Shops in which all work is on consignment have little capital invested in stock and can theoretically offer a higher profit to the artists. However, the percentage taken by the shop varies from as low as 10 percent (in rare cases) to as much as 50 percent. A 30 to 33 percent commission seems average and reasonable. The shops that take the smallest percentage are often craft studios, supply shops, or workshop studios; having work on display is an asset to the business. They show the work as attractive "eye catchers," knowing they will not necessarily sell well. So if you are paying a very small consignment fee, you may be getting small sales potential in return. Those craftsmen who outright reject all consignment should consider that all fine arts and professional galleries, of course, are run on what amounts to the same thing as consignment. An example of consignment at its best can be seen in outlets such as Julie:Artisan's Gallery Inc. in New York. Work is carefully screened and selected, so this is a case where being chosen to have work on consignment becomes a distinction. The shop functions as a showcase. Another consignment gallery/shop, Dabadaba, in Albany, California, finds ample response from artists. The owner comments that "artists have responded well because they know their work will be shown with other high-quality work." So the system itself may be all right—it is the abuses of it that are unacceptable, and the craftsman is often the one to lose out when things do go wrong.

Because a shop has no investment in them, items on consignment are not always well treated; small articles suffer the most. They get shopworn and occasionally are pilfered. Some shop owners are not interested in problems of damage and loss. So, working with someone you know will be your greatest asset, otherwise, check with other artists who have dealt with the shop in question. You must balance the advantages of having work shown against the ravages of dust, fading, handling, and theft.

It is advisable to set a time limit on all consigned work. Make an inventory list and get it signed. Find out who is responsible for damage or thefts and how you determine if a piece has been sold or if it "mysteriously disappeared." Have a clear understanding with the shop owner regarding the consignment percentage as well as how to handle special orders. Will you do them at all? Does your percentage remain the same? Discuss the length of time the work will be left, how it will be displayed, make sure that it *will* be displayed and not kept in a storeroom. Will you get designer credit for your work, and in what form? Will there be advertising or publicity? Various arrangements are possible, and you will have to handle each situation separately. If your work is greatly in demand you are in a better position to bargain. If you are desperate to have your work shown, you may accept less than satisfactory terms; you can always renegotiate. Most of us sell through consignment while getting started. Sometimes shops, too, are just starting in business, and the arrangements can change as either or both of you become better established. I personally have had good experiences in consignment.

When shops deal only with consigned works, the arrangements seem far better for the artists than when only a few things are on consignment. First, that shop-owner *must* have a good working relationship established with artists or craftsmen or he or she would be out of business. Record keeping (a hassle with consignment) will have been resolved. Most of these shops are also very selective, since there is a tremendous amount of fiber and fabric work available from which they can choose. That means your work won't be hung next to plastic mother-of-pearl combs from Taiwan. Having your work displayed in a good consignment gallery can be an honor, as well as financially worthwhile.

Cooperative galleries are usually able to take a much lower cut of sales than regular galleries. In return, they often require that you donate time to assist in running the gallery. That must be considered a cost on your part. Co-ops are often less efficient, since the members run the gallery, usually on a rotating basis. Some members are better at handling sales, more responsive to buyers, and more responsible salespeople than others. Co-ops keep you in touch with other producing craftsmen who have problems similar to yours, and they do provide space for exhibition and sale.

Co-ops vary so much that it is difficult to make any generalizations about them. They *are* well worth investigating, especially when you are getting started. Most artists do, at some time, belong to a co-op.

Direct sales offer good possibilities, with some drawbacks. Avoiding the middle man means more profit to you. It may mean increased sales because you can keep prices lower. It also means you must handle all the paper work, make contacts, return phone calls, handle money, open your studio or show area or attend fairs and sales. Selling takes time.

When you are ready to sell, tell people. Tell your friends, your relatives—everyone you know. So often craftsmen overlook the most obvious possible buyers. Sales in homes are surprisingly popular and very successful. Years ago I participated in sales with friends. We showed and sold our work for a weekend at someone's home. Eventually, the mailing lists got too long and parking turned into a nightmare. Knowing how to set limits is difficult.

Selling at fairs and craft shows has become a way of life for many producing craftsmen. Each fair is governed by its own regulations and has its own atmosphere or flavor. Check on what's available in your local area first. You'll learn very fast how to manage. Other craftspeople are a good source of information, although most fairs have printed regulations and suggestions for participants. Magazine articles and newspaper articles have covered many of the details of local shows.

Finally, women must help each other in terms of sales. If we all make sure that gifts and remembrances are purchased from friends, budding craftswomen and other artists, we can offer tremendous support and encouragement to each other. If you know someone who sews or paints or pots, purchase her work to give as gifts. The department store will survive without your patronage—the beginning craftsman may not.

Executing commissions is, for me, the most exciting way of working. There is challenge always, and some degree of tension. Most commissioned works require that you function essentially as a designer—that is, the work must be conceived and developed in terms of certain structural requirements. You plan within the limitations, to develop the maximum potential.

Not everyone wants to work on a commission basis. Some fiber artists prefer to do their own work as they please and sell it as buyers come along. Commissions have the advantage of being sold before the work is done. But doing commissions means working with a deadline, and in cooperation with other designers, with predetermined requirements of size, scale, or color. Commissions for private homes may be difficult if you feel as I do—when I'm asked to do a panel to match the sofa, my interest cools pretty rapidly. On the other hand, some clients show their responsiveness to your work by asking for your ideas of what's right. Find out whether commissions work well for you. Don't make any assumptions until you've tried working this way.

Barbara Murdock, for instance, has found:

I cannot work on a commission basis. The minute I know that I am making something for someone (even a friend) I begin to try to see it through their eyes and I feel tight and restricted—the product is almost always a flop and I begin to feel a resentment to myself, to the project, and to the person involved.

I enjoy commissions primarily because they often give me an opportunity to work on a large scale. Commissions through an architect or interior designer are likely to be for commercial buildings and public spaces. The opportunities for showing large works are otherwise limited.

Commissions usually develop through contact and exposure. If you read about a proposed construction, you can pursue that as a possibility, and contact the architect or interior planner. Or the architect or designer who is familiar with your work may call you and describe the job. If you can look at the actual building, do so, but blueprints or photos may have to serve if distance makes a first-hand view impractical, or if the building is not built as yet.

Next, you make a reasonably accurate scale sketch of your general idea. It may be in pen and ink, colored markers, tissue-paper collage, or any method that suits you. When you present the sketch to someone who does not know your work, it is very helpful to have with you photos, slides, or swatches of your work. These help to establish a direction for the work and assures that you are communicating. (How do you describe knotless netting or transparent appliqué to someone unfamiliar with them?) One example is worth a thousand explanations. If you can't make the presentation of your work in person, sending an example or a model with your proposal may be helpful. With your proposal, include samples of materials and indicate your awareness of fire codes, if they apply. (Some states require that any fiber or fabric hung on the wall of a public building must be fireproof. Any finished work can be treated to make it fire- or flameproof; check the Yellow Pages for a local processer.)

Your proposal and sketch usually must include an estimate of cost. Although some people balk at telling you what they have budgeted, I prefer to have a figure set by the client before I do any drawing: even a rough estimate helps. Otherwise, you can spend hours working on a proposal only to find that your estimate either is double or half of what your client intends to spend.

Your proposal should also include your estimate of the working time you will need (see Chapter 8 for a discussion of this).

Some artists require a retainer before they'll do a sketch or proposal. If the client has contacted you, you may be in a position to expect the retainer. (The retainer paid for a proposal is usually included as part of the total payment if you get the commission.)

The process of submitting sketches, getting approval, and finally starting work may take months. It may require two or three proposals to secure the commission, depending upon whether the architect or designer seeks your work, or you are offering your ideas in competition with other designers. (Because of the time involved when you work on commissions, it is important to keep more than one kettle on the stove.)

Once your proposal is ready, submit it in person and try to get an immediate response. If that is not possible, set a time when you will pick it up or a date by which you want it returned. Much of your most demanding work is in planning and designing, so a proposal represents much thought and effort. Let the client know that you value it enough to want your work back. Its return also prevents the client from passing your design or plan along to someone who will reproduce it at a lower estimate—which has happened to me. This denies the value of your design efforts. Receiving a retainer also helps avoid this, since an investment has been made in the design work.

I usually reserve the right to make changes from the model as I find them necessary for the visual or aesthetic success of the piece. The model is merely a guide— the work develops as it grows, and sometimes the model becomes only the starting point. Most architects and designers understand this. The important thing is to keep communicating, keep people informed, and send progress photographs or have the client visit your studio if necessary. Any problems can be caught early and misunderstandings avoided.

If you install your own work you may need to be aware of building codes that govern permanently mounted work, and wall structures which would determine the type of installation. The architect or engineer can be consulted on this.

Because commissions are often for commercial buildings, some recognition usually accompanies their installation. Recognition and the resulting reputation should lead you to greater freedom in selecting the most desirable jobs. Seeking commissions, however, is time consuming, often involving one in politics, meetings, proposals, concessions, and pressures of various kinds. It does not usually provide a Utopian solution for the artist or designer. However, it is an area to be investigated to determine if it is an appropriate approach for you.

Designing

Selling your designs offers a good potential for self-support. You may design either for production (manufacturing companies) or for magazines.

If you are interested in designing for production, familiarize yourself with what is on the market. One important area is kit design, and the range of kits available now includes many well-designed ones.

Write the companies for whom you feel your work would be most appropriate. Make an appointment to show your portfolio. Do not mail originals directly to any company. If you are asked to send work, send photographs or slides. Show the actual pieces in person, if at all possible.

If a company wishes to use your work they may either purchase outright or pay you on a royalty basis. Most designers prefer a royalty (a percentage of the selling price) for each kit, packet, or design sold, although this involves more book keeping for the manufacturer. The combination of a smaller direct payment plus a royalty is ideal. If a company makes no initial payment and then later decides not to produce a particular design, the artist will receive *no* compensation for her work. She will, in effect, have given the design away. If an initial payment in addition to a royalty is not a possibility, the artist should then set a time limit. For example, agree that if the design is not produced within a given time the design will revert to you for possible sale elsewhere.

Some companies supply all the materials for your designs since they must be able to duplicate what you select. Your original examples may have to be adapted for production; the number of colors may have to be limited, or the stitches simplified. Have a clear understanding of how the design will be altered, what will be required of you in terms of changes, and what control you will have over changes the company decides to make in your work. Further, a commitment regarding designer credit should be made at this point.

Many manufacturing companies buy designs from freelance artists. Take stock of your own interests and abilities, then try to match your work to the appropriate company. Even companies which have a staff of their own designers still buy good ideas outright.

All kinds of companies purchase free-lance, including those who manufacture toys, fabrics, wall papers, rugs, wrapping papers, sheets, books, album covers, needlepoint kits, clothes, and others. Fiber work can be photographed for printing on note paper, gift wraps, and fabric. Some children's books are illustrated with needlework. Even *Time* magazine has featured appliqué. Graphic artist Ann Ramos's fabric creations have been used in advertising. Needlepoint is frequently photographed for use in ads, and a recent billboard promotion featured soft sculpture. If you have good ideas, there is a market for them.

The most difficult step is in establishing an initial contact. Once that is done, your rapport with a company will grow as they get to know your work. After a couple of successful transactions, everything goes infinitely more smoothly.

There is also the heady possibility of starting your own kit business. Numerous women, often working in teams, have done this. Many bog down over distribution, but you can hire a representative to handle and distribute work on a percentage basis. Little companies pop up and disappear with remarkable speed and regularity. A few thrive; in others the enthusiasm burns off after the first few orders. Some sell only through mail order, others through retail shops.

If you are considering a business of this type, take advantage of the help that is available. Talk to someone already in the business, if possible. Community colleges and women's centers often offer courses on starting and running a small business. Your library will have books and other references available. The government printing office has many informative pamphlets. Magazine articles, which can be located through your library's Readers' Guide to Periodicals, are another good source of information.

Designing for magazines is always varied, challenging, and satisfying. It pays reasonably well (you may be paid more for the design than you would receive for selling the same item outright). However, it is demanding work in terms of deadlines. And you are sometimes credited in such small print that you need a magnifying glass to find your name.

Most magazines that use craft material have themes or overall plans for each issue, and each needlework editor has a group of designers with whom she usually works, contacting them regarding specific needs. Magazine editors do not ordinarily purchase ideas or items submitted "over the transom" (unsolicited) unless they happen to fit a particular theme. The editors do depend, of course, on new ideas and are great consumers of fabric and fiber arts of all kinds.

As with any prospective client, first write to the magazine (to the crafts or needlework editor). Send a short query letter along with a sample of your work (photocopies, color prints, or photos—not originals).

Family Circle's Deborah Harding requests a letter and photographs:

Photographs do not have to be professional; Instamatic or Polaroid is fine, color is helpful. Letter should contain basic background information, availability, experience, etc. If there is something of interest I will usually telephone and talk to the person and perhaps then request a sample of completed work. If it is a local artist, I will try to find the time to visit her studio. It is a waste of time to drop in unannounced; there is seldom anyone available to review work and it only creates confusion.

One editor of a women's magazine with a tremendous circulation says "presentation is not important" to her. She is looking for ideas:

We do emphasize originality and craftsmanship, but we also will buy an original idea and have it executed by someone else (with the designer's permission, of course). This we will do if the basic idea is good but the designer is not technically skilled to execute the project or does not have the time.

On the other hand, another editor comments that her major criticism of work submitted "is its presentation. We often get really bad photographs and poorly written instructions. Most artists don't seem to know how to present their ideas to a publisher." Margo Garrity, an editor of *Better Home and Gardens* annuals, also deplores

incomplete or inaccurate how-to directions. I always try to stress that good how-to should read like a recipe, i.e. with a list of materials (ingredients) followed by step-to-step directions. Always include patterns or sketches, if needed. Never submit directions in long hand. They should be double-spaced, typewritten. Each item should be on a separate page, with name and address at the top of each page.

Designing for magazines entails the writing of directions for your design. That means knowing exact yardage, writing cutting instructions, diagrams for the work, drawings for patterns, and explanations. These will be rewritten by the magazine staff, but it is imperative that your writing be clear and concise. I find it's often more difficult to write directions for a piece than to just *do* the work!

If your work is sensational, a magazine will probably buy it, even plan an article around it. No magazine will disregard something so spectacular that it would send the women of America careening down the streets for the grocer's newest issue of that magazine. But not every piece of work sets the magazine world on fire, and a great work of art is not necessarily suitable for magazine use. As Deborah Harding says,

The biggest problem with fine artists is the discipline required to adapt to commercial interests. It is important to do adequate research and keep precise notes for how-tos. You can't use beautiful one-of-a-kind fabric finds or make a quilt with every square different if it's necessary to publish patterns in the magazine.

Read the magazines and see what kind of work they include. Remember that they want designs with a wide range of appeal. If your three-year-old has her baby-talk version of Jack and Jill, that may be perfect on a quilt for her. But not everyone is going to share your enthusiasm for her cute little speech imperfections.

Magazine editors have a consistently positive view of the future for women in designing for the fiber arts. Deborah Harding states that there is

a definite spiralling interest in all areas of fiber arts and in all spectrums of society and genera-tions. Young people are educated and appreciative of handmade arts. Society ladies who used to do needlepoint as a noblesse oblige *pastime are now elbow deep in dyeing their own yarns. Pedestrian household items handmade out of economic necessity have new dimensions as art forms. Fortunately, I see fewer "plastic-dipped flower" type crafts and more and more really good quality patchwork, appliqué, crochet and more inventive kinds of rugs. Cross-stitch, counted and drawn thread work, as well as Blackwork, are popular again. Most women (and men) are more likely to spend time and money on something that will be functional and decorative. Usually, accessories for the home.*

Mollie Kerr, editor of *Fibernews*, says, "The future has many possibilities and we are only in our infant stages now. Women artists are starting to see themselves as professionals and to approach work this way."

Marilyn Heise, who publishes *Working Craftsman*, feels there is: ". . . more com-petition each year. Originality and style are becoming more important."

Fees for magazine design work vary. If your work is commissioned by a magazine, it will usually command a higher price than if you have submitted unsolicited work. Some magazines pay designers on the same basis as graphic artists—that is, in terms of the page size or the space covered in the published work (quarter-page, half-page, full-page, color page, etc.). Others may pay a set fee, which may or may not take into account the space and kind of use, the complexity of the item, its originality, or your reputation. *What* you furnish—just an idea, or finished samples and directions—may also be the basis for payment. Some magazines pay for major mate-rials you need to buy, or for postage (be sure to keep your receipts for these cases).

Fredrica Daugherty, editor-in-chief of *Decorating and Craft Ideas*, says: "We negotiate on the basis of just how much the artist furnishes. For example if we just buy an idea we pay less than if we are furnished samples and a story."

Gertrude Dieken, at *Countryside Living* and *Farm Journal*, says this magazine has no established pay scale. She adds, "Depends on originality, craftsmanship, whether items must be mailed in for us to photograph or whether photos are available, the intended use, space in the magazine, and whether it's used individually or as part of a mixup in the photos."

Payment may be made either for the article itself or for the photographic and design rights. Find out which method of payment is used before you agree to a fee. If work is purchased outright, you send in your work, you receive a check, and that's that. Once you send the work off you won't see it again, except as it appears in print. If the magazine purchases design and photographic rights, you send your finished work in for photography. After the issue in which the article appears is published, it will be returned to you. You can then use it, exhibit it, or sell it. You cannot, of course, make any further commercial or published use of the design. If you later want to photograph it for use in some other publication, you must obtain permission from the magazine. Some magazines buy all photographic rights, others purchase only first photographic rights.

Some publications do not pay anything for your work, either because they are non-profit-making or because they are small or new publications that are working on a slim margin. They depend heavily upon contributions by craftsmen. Often this is a trade of sorts, in which the contributing craftsman gains exposure to a selected group of readers. Even some large commercial magazines don't pay; as Alyson Smith Gonsalves of Sunset Books points out:

Merely publishing the work of an artist can be (and often is) construed to be a fair payment in the form of free publicity. However, the artist is the one whose time, energy and creativity have gone into the production of the art works submitted to us for final publication selection. While our contribution is to attempt a careful, tasteful and exciting selection of work. . . . which will hopefully inspire and educate the public, without the contributing artists we can't function. They are essential to our success.

What you are paid for magazine work *is* influenced by the attitude that such designing is "women's work." One magazine associate editor made this blunt comment:

Money and management positions for women in the fiber arts are not commensurate with conditions for men. Many times a writer will get paid more for a 30-minute interview with a TV "star" or politician's offspring than a designer will get for several months of work on a quilt or rug design as it's still thought of as "women's work" by men—especially in publishing. There are also occasions where a photographer will come in and earn as much in a day or two to photograph a room or series of designs that may have taken an editor and/or artist half a year to research and develop. Also, decision-making positions in all major yarn and fabric manufacturers, kit companies, magazines and catalogs are controlled by men. There's still a long way to go to get beyond token woman executives.

All magazine editors look for a combination of craftsmanship and originality. Deborah Harding puts this succinctly:

Most of the submissions I receive are not original. Frequently people even send me my own magazine ideas or a design from a kit or book, feeling that because they "made it," it's "theirs." This is the biggest problem among amateurs.

Copying—intentional and unintentional, is a problem that is not confined to magazine work. I was once contacted by a company that wanted to commission a cover for their menu cards. They brought me an example of one that had been very popular. They already had my work on the cover! Inside, the designer credit named the person who had executed the yarn-embroidered daisies from a pattern I had designed for a national magazine. The "designer" probably thought it was her work—after all, she paid for the pattern and sewed it! The panel, of course, was hers, but the design was not, and it was unethical and unprofessional of her to sell it.

A fabric company printed ersatz quilt-patterned fabric which is copied from one of my books (they drew in all the stitches—in perfectly awful colors!). Copies of quilts I made for my own children have won awards and prizes for other women; one is reproduced without credit to me in a quilt book now on the market. In another case, I made a quilt-block appliqué showing a telephone with only five numbers on it, because that was how far my son could count at that time. All the copies of it include five-number telephones! Such copies miss the essence of the design and the maker's personal involvement in it. I'm told that imitation is a form of flattery. Many women, accustomed to patterns and kits, do not understand that designing doesn't just mean following the directions. I forgive them. But if you design for publication of any kind, be prepared for this.

In magazine work, patterns are often sold by the magazine, but you will always know ahead of time of that arrangement. I once exhibited a quilt which I had designed for the cover of *Family Circle*. A woman came into the exhibition and (since she had ordered the pattern to make one like it) exclaimed, "Oh look, there's a copy of my quilt!" This doesn't upset me—of course she thinks of it as her quilt, she made one. . . . and that *is* a tradition in quilting, to make and exchange patterns.

When your ideas are sold by someone else or win prizes for others, you will feel infringed upon. As Kathy Vidak expresses it:

I always have felt I was being egotistical when I put a price on my work and expected people to buy it. My change of attitude was helped along when people from my classes began to take my ideas and techniques and sell them. That made me mad. Especially when, many times, they were awfully poor copies!!! So, now I sell my own ideas myself!

One way of protecting your work is to copyright it. This is a very simple process involving registration of the work you want protected with the U.S. Copyright Office. For complete information on copyrighting, write the Copyright Office, Library of Congress, Washington, D.C. 20559. The February '77 issue of *Craft Horizons* has an article entitled New Copyright Law Aids Artists, which offers concise and helpful information. Copyrighting does not solve all problems and it cannot eliminate the "borrowing" or "adapting" of your ideas. It is definitely helpful if you are marketing production pieces.

Teaching

Teaching frequently provides income for fiber artists. If you are a college or university teacher, you can sometimes specialize in the fiber area, although you may also teach art, art education, home economics, experimental classes, feminist programs, folk-life studies, summer sessions and extension courses. If you are not already teaching and have a class or course idea, contact the appropriate department, the director of extension, summer sessions, continuing education, etc. Call high schools, junior highs, community colleges, state colleges, and universities. While community colleges and secondary schools require certain educational degrees, they also have flexibility for special programs. Universities can hire more on the basis of unusual talent, although if you have no graduate degree you may only be eligible on a semester basis. Recreation and art centers, Ys, and adult-education organizations all offer an ever-expanding range of classes.

Beatrice Sheftel says:

Seeing the desire of many women to pursue an interest in crafts, but needing training, I contacted the town about organizing voluntary craft classes. . . . the director of recreation hired me to organize and run the craft program. I started women's programs as the only teacher. I taught knitting, crochet, macramé, crewel, needlepoint, quilting and creative crafts that first year. Then gradually I ran classes with specialists in different fields, mainly other women whose hobbies had grown into professions.

Even if you have expertise in just one area, you may find you can offer a course; many teaching aids are available. Public and school libraries have books which cover more than everything you or your students may need to know. Slides are available through museums and galleries. Special-interest publications, crafts magazines and books list sources for all kinds of visual aids. Remember too that senior-citizen centers often house women with needlework talents; visit them and invite them to share their work in a class. This kind of input broadens the range of your class, exposes you to new ideas, and certainly recognizes the experienced needlewoman.

The advantage of teaching through a structured education program is that facilities are provided and advertising or promotion are taken care of, leaving you free to teach. Adult-education programs often pay according to the number of students enrolled, in which case you may find yourself involved in recruiting. Other programs pay by the hour or by the class.

Teaching at home is another possibility; I found it both enjoyable and profitable. You can schedule classes while the children are in school. Though class size must be limited according to your work space, all your examples, aids, and materials are right at hand. There is no hauling or commuting. The atmosphere is casual and non-threatening to the most hesitant stitcher. Also, teaching at home can pay better than teaching where the class fee must also pay for the building, the janitorial service or the secretarial and mailing help. On the other hand, you must strictly limit the time your students spend with you; they tend to linger. One way is to arrange classes to end with the arrival of your children, say from 10 to 12 noon. At 12:10 a hungry six-year-old bursts in the door and it pretty much ends the class.

I loved teaching at home, but not everyone does. It means getting breakfast dishes off the table early and having a presentable bathroom and some clean towels. It means handling scheduling, finances, and advertising, but you also get to stay home.

Besides teaching through schools or teaching at home there are good opportunities for teaching through stitchery groups, embroidery guilds, and needlework shops. One-day workshops are sometimes a good solution if you don't mind going out of town. Shops often prefer once-a-week-for-six-weeks sessions.

Whatever kind of teaching you undertake, be sure to clarify the details ahead of time. Be sure to consider these: How will you be paid—by the student, the hour, the class, or the session? Under what circumstances will the class be canceled? By what date? What publicity or advertising will be done for the class? Who will handle the registration and collection of fees? Who opens the building or takes care of the room? Will you be paid at the beginning or the completion of the course or periodically? Will you be reimbursed for travel? Is there a *per diem* allowance if you are to be away from home overnight? Universities and colleges usually have a simple contract that covers these questions. If none is provided, you may write out your own. If you do not use a contract (I don't for guild workshops or for lectures), it is a good idea to have a confirming letter that clarifies the arrangements.

Besides offering a good supplemental source of income to fiber artists, teaching can also give much pleasure through sharing and watching talents develop. Teaching forces you to organize your thoughts and your materials. You become more aware of your own work processes as you explain them to someone else. If you are to be a good teacher, you must be willing to share. Anyone who feels protective of her ideas or her work is probably not ready to teach. It is true that students in their first tentative explorations may do work similar to the teacher's—or may actually copy. It's an indication of their insecurity. Help them to grow into their own work. Often the woman who copies is groping—she needs something to hang on to. Being creative is frightening to women who have not done it before. If you are teaching only techniques, this problem is not so acute—students feel more at ease there. It's when they have to make aesthetic decisions that they become overwhelmed with their choices.

Lecturing

For me, one of the most enjoyable aspects of lecturing is the opportunity to talk to women in the fiber arts and to see first hand what is going on in various parts of the country. The women I meet are remarkable and interesting, and some have become lasting friends. I also enjoy the travel.

Audiences of fiber artists are particularly warm, responsive, and accepting. They are unlikely to judge you by the style of your hairdo or look for high fashion in your clothes. I find it's not necessary to perform; I can be me.

If you are ready to lecture, try a small group first. I was so petrified before my first talk I thought I'd never utter an intelligible word. It gets easier. If you find you are comfortable with a small group, then contact various other organizations. Speakers bureaus and convention bureaus often look for speakers. Write to groups and clubs, describing your field. Get lists of clubs through chambers of commerce, libraries, newspapers, craft publications. When you find one or two you are on your way. To get started and to gain experience you might volunteer a program for your mother's club or for a league you are involved in or for your own PTA. The first talk is definitely the hardest, and others will grow out of that.

I have never actively looked for speaking engagements, and I do not use an agency. Requests come to me primarily because of my books and my exhibitions. Word of mouth is the best advertising there is, so there is lots of free advertising in this field! Everytime you lecture you greatly increase the prospects for another engagement, because members of the audience often contact you to speak for their groups.

You can make lecture arrangements directly with the sponsoring group. Lecture/workshops are often arranged for by several groups in an area so that they can cut expenses by sharing the travel cost, though each pays its own workshop and lecture fees. Sometimes guilds combine efforts with a university, or two organizations share a lecture. Museums or galleries often cosponsor lectures.

Most of my lecturing has been for fiber guilds, woman's clubs of all kinds (from the Association of American University Women to dental auxiliaries), community colleges, city or county schools (programs for teachers), women's-study and artist-in-residence programs, and national seminars and conferences.

Experience will teach you to set limits on the time you agree to be away from home (and your own work). Two weeks is the longest trip I've made, and I prefer one week (after ten days I seem to have less patience for questions which have already been answered twice).

Most groups will make reasonable demands on time and energy. Only occasionally do they schedule a class, a TV interview, a dinner, a lecture, and a book-signing all in one day. Time to yourself is crucial—time to relax, put your feet up, and read your notes, etc. Lecturing is hard work, and a series of lectures can be exhausting. But I find it rewarding. My greatest pleasure is in doing my own work; sharing it with others comes next.

Sponsoring groups often invite you to stay as house guest with a member of the group, as this cuts their costs. Some lecturers prefer to stay at a hotel, finding the home entertaining too tiring. Others love staying in individual homes. I usually go along with whatever a group suggests—there are advantages in either arrangement.

I find it helpful to make generous amounts of carefully selected visual material available at every lecture. To do so takes me from one to three days of preparation for each talk (not counting doing the original work and making slides of the pieces you wish to show). A lecture is really an accumulation of many years' work. The lecture itself is usually given extemporaneously, but having an outline or notes available is reassuring.

A ton of luggage seems to be required to assure a wide range of examples for students to see. I plan carefully for a lecture, and feel infinitely more confident than I did at first. Even so, lecturing is not a breeze. And any lecturer must allow for a few foulups. Projector bulbs burn out, or the projectionist doesn't show up (thought it was next Wednesday!). Newspapers misprint the date of the lecture, or someone forgets to tell the custodian and the door to the lecture room is still locked as people arrive. Most fiber groups are not greatly experienced in offering lecturers and some details may be overlooked. So it is important to stay loose, know that everyone *wants* it all to go smoothly, and will help in every way possible. It is helpful to set up for a lecture well ahead of lecture time. That way most of the bugs can be eliminated before you begin.

Once you feel confident about lecturing, it's important to establish a fee. You must take into consideration whether your travel expenses, if any, will be reimbursed. When I am invited to speak, I offer to mail an information sheet which gives my fees, the subjects for lecture, and workshop outlines. Establishing a fee does not mean you cannot volunteer your services when you wish. Send your fee schedule and indicate "no charge" if you like, or ask the group to make a donation to a charity you select. But identify it as an exception. It is not fair to your self or to other craftswomen and artists to let any organization, however worthy, assume that your time has no value. If you belong to the organization, you may want to waive your fee. If you want to contribute your fee to the group, do so. But you should not feel embarrassed to accept a check for your services.

Writing

Writing books on crafts does not ordinarily fill a pot of gold at the end of the royalty rainbow and allow the fiber artist to retire. The competition is keen, both in publication and in sales. But there are obvious benefits, too.

Writing is hard work. But assuming you still want to write a book, here are some considerations.

First, acquaint yourself with the books already available in your field. Be familiar with publishers and the kinds of books they have done. Next, determine whether or not you have something new or different to offer, if your approach is innovative, or your method of presenting the material is distinct. There is no point in simply doing again what has already been well done. Publishers are not interested in material that has already been published.

Once you have determined that your idea is valid, consider whether it is marketable. Sometimes a single idea makes a superb pamphlet or magazine article but is not suitable for a book. Is there enough interest, a wide enough audience, to justify its publication? Is the assumed audience teachers, school children, professionals, or homemakers? Be realistic about the range of appeal and the limitations of your particular approach.

The first step in finding a publisher is to work up an outline. Determine the scope and the sequence of the book. Write it down, and compose a paragraph describing each chapter. That gives you the skeleton. The rest is the muscle or the body, and that's where the fun begins.

Write letters of inquiry to appropriate publishers (don't send a book on quilting to a publisher who specializes in Gothic novels). Explain briefly what your proposed book is about and enclose a resume. Suggest that if they are interested you will send your proposal and outline. (I know of at least two authors of fiber-arts books who finished their entire manuscripts before writing a publisher. Each felt very secure about her work and in what she was doing, and plunked the entire manuscript down on the publisher's desk. Complete. And had it accepted. If you feel less confident than this, submit your proposal in advance.)

In the proposal packet you send off to a prospective publisher you should include your tentative title, outline, chapter headings, one sample chapter or a portion of a chapter (to assure them that you can write a coherent sentence), and two or three examples of whatever visual material you plan to use (photographs, drawings, or diagrams). Send only good-quality work—photos and finished drawings or diagrams that you consider appropriate for the published work. It doesn't do to say, "This is a rough sketch but I can do better." Do better.

Don't be discouraged by a rejection. Be ready to send your proposal right off to another publisher. Publishers are increasingly selective in the crafts field, but one editor may see potential where another does not. One editor says she hopes to see "fewer and better books at all levels."

Another editor felt a need for books at both extremes—fine-art-type books in the crafts, and good beginner-level books. Others see an increase in sophistication and a growing enthusiasm for experimentation in new craft media and new techniques. And another commented, "I believe this area of craft books will remain very strong . . . especially in the area of self expression. The number of books may decrease."

My sister Jackie Vermeer's first book (on preschooler's crafts) was rejected by seven different publishers. A few wrote encouraging letters, others sent form letters, but all responded promptly. Totally discouraged, she mailed it unenthusiastically to the eighth publisher, who said it was exactly what the company had been looking for. So you can see what you might be missing if you drag your heels after just *four* rejections! Persistence pays off. Sometimes a publisher will consider a book that was rejected a year earlier. The climate for books changes.

Alyson Smith Gonsalves says:

Don't be afraid to take the chance with a publisher; a rejection slip is not the end of the world. Keep trying until you run out of publishers—then revamp your manuscript and polish it up. . . . and send it out again. Getting publishers to remember who you are takes work, but it can pay off. Be as brief and as pleasant as possible. A pleasant but persistent approach will help you a great deal.

Terry Taplinger, of Taplinger Publishing Company, has a positive attitude about new authors:

We have been delighted to discover that many amateur needleworkers and craftspeople have the capacity to write first-rate, exciting books—even without prior writing experience. We welcome direct contact with such craftsmen all over the country and are happy to encourage their efforts where feasible.

The editors I know are unanimous in their willingness to review manuscripts. Each preferred an initial contact by letter, then the combination of outline, synopsis, and visuals described earlier.

I have worked with four different book publishers and have enjoyed getting to know some marvelous editors at each. All are women (which seems to be the norm in crafts) and all have been open, fair, and helpful. I count several among my good and most interesting friends. I have learned a lot through experience, and am surprised to look back now and realize what a chance my first publisher took on an unknown, unpublished young craftswoman who was doing work that seemed at the time to be way off the beaten track.

It is more difficult to make demands when you are an unknown writer. You're always in a better bargaining position on a second book, if your first one is a success. You do need a publisher before you can get your book out (unless you are one of the few who publish themselves), but publishers, remember, also need writers. You are mutually dependent.

If a publisher likes your idea and decides to publish your book, you'll get a contract, which usually provides, among other things, for a delivery date for the material and for payment. You do not have to either accept or reject the contract—much of it is negotiable. You may find it helpful to have the assistance of a contract attorney (they work on a fee basis rather than a percentage, like an agent) or to consult with someone who has written books. Or you may decide to use a literary agent. Fiber artists have varying attitudes about agents. Some would not venture into any contract without the aid of an agent, others simply would not work through one at all. There are advantages and disadvantages (depending on whom you talk to) and you must weigh the merits of either in terms of your own abilities or needs.

An agent usually asks 10 percent of your royalty (and advance) as a fee. The agent may be able to negotiate a higher royalty, but you also have higher costs. Talk to an agent, ask what he or she can offer you before deciding. An agent is familiar with publishing houses, contracts, and the details of business arrangements. Some artists are greatly relieved to have this taken off their hands, but others want to be directly involved. Florence Pettit says:

I do not have and never will have an agent. It never occurred to me in the beginning, and hasn't seemed necessary since. I know I've had my share of pure dumb luck, but I think believing in a book and being able to put it across personally has been of help. I've done only two books (the childrens') on a contract signed in advance. The three adult books I've done first, and signed the contract when I delivered the whole fat package ... having only a verbal acceptance in the beginning. I don't think there is any "best" way to do it. Some people shrink from the idea of having to sell themselves, or don't want to spend the time. I think the only thing that matters is to do it the way you are convinced is best for you. You can have bad luck with or without an agent, too.

I have never worked with an agent, but my contracts seem as good or better than some I know of that were handled by agents. When I had my first dealings with a publisher, I didn't know there *were* agents for people like me. I sailed on by without one.

You can expect to receive 10 percent royalty on hardbound books, though a range from 6 percent to 12 percent, depending on other variables, is possible; the royalty on paperbacks is somewhat lower. Some publishers pay on a sliding scale, so that if a book sells well, your royalties escalate. For instance, your royalty may be 10 percent on the first 5,000 (or 7,500 or 10,000) copies sold, but rise to 12½ percent after that and (more rarely) to 15 percent after another 5,000 copies.

The cost of photography and providing drawings and diagrams is usually considered the craft author's responsibility, although sometimes publishers will contribute to the expense of making or obtaining illustrations. (If you can't or don't choose to provide illustrations, another person may be chosen and may share in your royalties. One author said her illustrator receives 2½ percent to her 7½ percent: Others receive 3 percent.) These areas are negotiable and you should not hesitate to ask for everything you want. The publisher will not hesitate to say no if he must. In those cases where the publisher takes care of photography you may receive a smaller royalty, since photo costs can be an expensive part of a book.

Publishers usually pay you an advance against royalties; this is based upon what your book is expected to earn, and is deducted from your royalty payments later. Only those payments designated as "grants" or as "outright payments" are not deducted. The advances vary greatly, usually being paid in installments—part upon signing of the contract, part upon receipt of finished manuscript, and sometimes part on publication. My advances have ranged from $500 to $4000, depending on the publisher and the particular book.

If illustrating rather than writing books interests you, contact publishers and ask if they will keep a portfolio of your work on file. (Not all publishers will accept portfolios.) Since good methods of making reproductions are available, it's possible to send out several such portfolios. A publisher will often help locate an illustrator for writers, and only if your portfolio is there on file can you be considered for that opportunity.

Illustrating artists may be paid outright or by royalty, depending in part on the importance of the drawings in the book. And an artist may be paid either by the writer or by the publisher. A royalty is preferable (unless the book doesn't sell!), but it is not always offered. In any case, the artist should have an advance.

Writing magazine articles about crafts is another good prospect for income. You may cover work of your own, write about the work of other artists, (with their permission, of course!), report on new techniques, and new directions. Always write a letter of inquiry first. Some publications produced by organizations do not pay for articles at all. You must decide for yourself if the publicity you gain compensates you for your time and talent.

Many feminist publications are open to articles, and they usually pay for work. Even if payment is small, it's a beginning. You need a backlog of experience and publication, and all exposure is valuable. If you are submitting work, start at the top with the best. Submit to your first choice first. If you are rejected, then try the next.

Remember finally that magazines and publishers *need* writers. They can't exist without continuously finding and using new material.

Joint Ventures

Few things expand one's courage and confidence so dramatically as working with someone else. It has been my experience that joint ventures are twice as much fun and half as much work.

Year ago, convinced that two fools will rush in where one will fear to tread, Ruth Law and I developed a small silk-screen printing company. The printing was done in our kitchens or garages, and paper stock was stored under beds and tables until it had its own room. The whole venture was fun and even if we didn't retire on the income, we did travel a little and enjoy some profit on our investment. She and I later co-authored *Handmade Toys and Games* and worked on several magazine articles together. With her I ventured into projects I'd never have tackled alone, and we were always able to bolster one another's courage when necessary.

I have written several books together with Joyce Aiken, and we also jointly run Everywoman's Studio, a workshop center for women in fiber arts. We have plunged headlong into commissions, completely undaunted by jobs that neither of us would have dared to undertake alone.

Because both of these experiences are among the ones I most treasure, I'm the first in line to recommend joint ventures. A strong, healthy respect for one another's work is crucial. There is a give and take in team work, and as work progresses each person seems to naturally take responsibility for the areas which she can handle best.

Joint ventures do not work well for everyone. Some people have encountered rough spots, and found that friendships survived, warmer and stronger than they were before; others have ended in lawsuits and bitterness. Working together, and usually with a deadline, adds pressure. It is a very intense time. But it is also exhilarating. If you get frustrated over one aspect of your work, your coworker can rescue you. You can do the same for her.

What the magic ingredients for success are I cannot tell. I only know that I would not have missed the co-operative ventures for anything.

It is important in any co-op effort to be sure you have the same goals, and that they are openly discussed. Each person must be willing to look at her own work critically and analyze her own contribution. Being able to admit your own inadequacies or errors is tremendous help. Most difficulties arise from disparities in terms of contribution. If one or the other feels an imbalance in the time or energy or talent that goes into the work, there will be trouble. Keeping all thoughts objective and in the open will help.

An advantage of joint undertakings is that they pool experience and expertise. (The business world is well aware of this!) So often it requires nothing short of courage to approach an architect or a publisher with an idea. Two can prop each other up. So many women have had little opportunity for experience in business; if this is an avenue that makes it easier for you, use it.

Group ventures also have great potential in shop situations. Many needlework centers, weaver's studios, yarn shops, and quilt stores are run by two, three, or more women. They all share the advantages and the fun, and no one has the full weight of responsibility, a real asset if you have children. June Steinbaugh offers this:

Three years ago, three friends and I started Weavers Workshop Ltd., a gallery/weaving supply shop where we exhibit our own work, sell looms, books, yarn, etc. and give classes. Our business is thriving and very gratifying. We are four women, all married, with a total of 12 children among us. We open our shop 10-3 Tuesday–Saturday and each work there two or three days a week. We receive no salary since all profits have been going back into the business. But we have a great variety of materials available to us and also an outlet for our work which we produce at home. . . .

Primarily I am a weaver but I started out 15 years ago making puppets for a friend who is a puppeteer. I still build entire puppet productions for the Puppet Playhouse and also individual puppets for TV on a free-lance basis. This work I do in my kitchen workshop at home.

Once you have provided yourself with some income, there is the exhilarating prospect of determining how to use it. Most women, even when they are making relatively little money, want first of all to cover their expenses.

Jackie Vermeer views her income in this way:

When I was starting and didn't make much, my goal was to at least try to support my "habit." I kept all the money I made and used it to buy supplies for whatever I was working on. Now that my income has increased, the money is mine for whatever I want.

Our arrangement is this: Lou has his job and that money goes for the household budget; if he does an extra job like weekend consulting, that money is his to keep. I do the housework and care and feeding of the family as my contribution to the home—any extra work or job that I do, that money is mine to keep. I certainly wouldn't squander the money if we needed it for the family budget, but at the same time, no one assumes it's available. This has been a really great arrangement, and I wouldn't do it any other way.

As income increases, there is the sheer joy of being able to do things for others with money you've earned. You can indulge in an occasional extravagant dinner out without feeling guilty for having depleted the week's grocery budget, or you can allow an eight-year-old an extra week at camp. As one artist stated, "Money frees me and puts me in control of an aspect of my life where I used to feel helpless."

When a fiber artist becomes self-supporting through her work, a mutually agreed-upon arrangement with her partner or family usually develops. This relates directly to family financial needs, of course. The artist's income is often sporadic, so a flexible system is needed. Both I and my husband free-lance, so we never have an *assured* income. This requires a very positive attitude, a good sense of humor, and sometimes a keen appreciation of meatloaf in various disguises. It's a feast-or-famine kind of existence which we enjoy but not everyone can tolerate. It is certainly more reassuring for an aspiring artist to have a spouse who holds down a steady job in what your relatives refer to as "real work."

Beth Gutcheon describes the fund-sharing system used in her home:

We each commit a certain amount of money to household and kid-related expenses each month. If in any given month either of us can sock away more than that amount, we each have a separate savings account. That means that if one of us wants to stop working for money for a while (as I would like to do, to make more quilts, or work on a novel) I must work ahead until I have saved enough to cover several months, and then I quit. At least, I plan to this winter; I've tried it a couple of times before but something always came up. Anyway, it's worked well for us, because neither one feels taken advantage of by the other, and neither one feels inferior to the other, and when I want to buy Jeffrey a new pair of socks or take him out to dinner, by god I have my own money and he knows he's having a real treat.

Another fiber artist adds:

The money my husband makes is our *money, but the money I make is* my *money. I keep a separate bank account and use my money for trips, Christmas, books, supplies, etc. I was so proud when I was finally able to buy my husband a birthday present that he didn't end up paying for.*

"Making it" in one's art offers tremendous pleasure. It helps erase feelings of insecurity or uncertainty about the present and the future. Knowing what you can do adds greatly to feelings of confidence and self-esteem.

There are pleasures, rewards, and challenges in being at home and in being with one's small children. But there are also great satisfactions in developing a thriving career and realizing one's potentials. I hope this book will help women to see how it is possible to have both.

I offer, finally, my warmest encouragement and support to the creative women currently involved in their own personal odysseys towards "getting-it-all-together-at-home."

Earning money gives me greater independence and it definitely increases my status at home. I think the more you get paid, the more you respect your own work. (Joyce Aiken)

For me, money is freedom. I like that. I enjoy the control it gives me over my own life. My husband respects my work more now, and the income justifies my use of studio space.

My income has steadily increased each year but not enough to fully support myself. As I managed more time for my work, I realized more shows, commissions and workshops. But it's taken many years of commitment, and hard work to arrive at this point. (Barbara Kensler)

I have learned that there is a lot of potential in me. My small ventures into school, independent business, and teaching are a constant surprise. I guess it speaks of the unsureness in me that I am so surprised and pleased with my successes. It really makes life interesting when you can constantly learn new things about yourself. This is what living is all about. (Jody House)

Life for me, for us, is exciting. I never know what's coming next. But one thing is for sure, things just get better and better. (Beatrice Sheftel)

Note

In the past few years changes have occurred in the kinds of questions asked of me in workshops and lectures. With craft books available to cover practically every known skill and technique, the questions now are about priority-setting, life goals, and the combining of career and home responsibilities. The questions most often asked formed the basis for my first thoughts on this book (see the questionnaire reproduced below).

Some of the questions make assumptions with which I do not agree—for example, "How do you keep your children out of your work?" Like "When did you stop beating your wife?" a situation is implicit in the question. Nevertheless, I asked the question this way for two reasons. First, it reveals a basic conflict of the woman working at home. Second, in discussing a practical, everyday situation, most women express a clear and strong philosophy about childrearing; many would withdraw from a purely philosophical question.

Similarly, being "confined" to the home is as much a state of mind as it is a physical situation. Anyone who can get to the library once a month has endless information at her disposal the rest of the time. If you have a phone, you have access to the world. So again, there is an underlying assumption in the question.

I can only emphasize that I have repeated the questions most often asked by mothers and young craftswomen. These are the terms in which they view the problems.

I wrote to nearly 150 fiber artists and other professional women regarding this book. A different questionnaire was sent out to editors at major book publishers, editors of crafts and women's magazines, and to gallery and shop owners, all of whom were women. The responses from them were often similar and consistent.

Almost all the craftswomen commented on the importance, to them, of writing down their answers. Several said that just having to sit down, think about the questions, and write made them see things more clearly, helped them to redefine goals and reset values. One woman said she had not written so much in the first person singular in twenty years. Two or three were disgruntled because the questions gobbled up an entire morning of valuable work time. A couple told me that they never filled out such questionnaires since their time was too important (though they proceeded to write long letters). Many actually thanked me, for they found that writing it down clarified what they were doing.

After reading the first 25 or 30 responses, I found that the remaining answers tended to repeat what was said in the first sampling, though each woman had her individual way of expressing her views. So the additional responses served to reinforce, but did not necessarily add significantly new dimensions. I assume from this that the opinions I quote speak for the most part for most craftswomen.

After the first responses came in, it became unnecessary to contact more women, and thus some well-known and much-admired fiber artists may not be represented. The paperwork became overwhelming, since most artists responded with *pages* rather than with a few lines. I found myself trying to limit the amount of incoming material rather than to expand it. As one friend commented regarding the voluminous answers, "We were overwhelmed and delighted to think there was someone who actually wanted to know what we thought!"

All the quotations in this book are from the women who responded to my questions. I have identified the individuals where it was possible.

"I do what I do because I have to. It's part of me. I could not survive without creative expression."

Eleanor A. Van de Water (Photographer: Darryl Johansen)

138

"It has gotten a lot easier as the kids have gotten older—more interested in doing it instead of eating it. When we were at Stanford living in student housing with four tinies I used to paint on top of the refrigerator so they couldn't get into it."

Mary Sprague (Photographer: Mary Ellen Elkins)

The questions:

1. How do you find time for your work and for your home?
   Do you?

2. Where do you find the space for your work?
   Do other members of the family have space for their work?

3. How do you store materials?

4. How can you do all these jobs and do them all well?
   How many hours in your day?

5. How do you keep children out of your work?
   Do you try?

6. What if your husband doesn't like all the mess and activity?

7. How do you manage when you have a deadline?

8. Is it possible to support yourself through your art or craft?
   Do you?
   Or could you if necessary?

9. Where do you get inspiration and ideas if you are confined to your home most of the time with children, cooking, and laundry?

My warmest thanks go to all the artists who so generously and willingly shared their thoughts (and fears), their experiences and their time, and to my friends:

B. J. Adams, fiber artist, Washington, D.C.
Joyce Aiken, teacher and designer, author of *Portable Needlepoint* and co-author of *The Total Tote Book*, Clovis, California
Carole Austin, designer, soft-sculpture artist, Orinda, California
Bonnie Bartell, exhibiting artist, Eugene, Oregon
Ethel Jane Beitler, stitchery artist, Lubbock, Texas
Helen Bitar, artist-craftsman, Portland, Oregon
Margot Carter Blair, designer, co-author of *The Banner Book: How to Sew a Celebration*, Mission Viejo, California
Diane Bower, home economist, college teacher, spinner, and quilter, Pebble Beach, California
Wilanna Bristo, artist/designer in needle arts, San Antonio, Texas
Elsa Brown, artist, teacher, and author of *Creative Quilting*, Richfield, Connecticut
Ginger Carter, designer and teacher, Frontenac, Missouri
Jane Chapman, teacher, fiber craftsman, La Mesa, California
Carole Clark, stitcher, Visalia, California
Ricky Clark, quiltmaker and stitcher, Oberlin, Ohio
Madge Copeland, textile artist and teacher, Sunnyvale, California
Linda Cross, craftswoman and co-author of *Kitchen Crafts,* New York, New York
Sally K. Davidson, designer and craftsman, Rochester, New York
Jenny DeBouzek, student, San Francisco, California
Ann deWitt, "heuristicist" and craftswoman, California
Jo Diggs, craftsman, Corrales, New Mexico
Rose Dwight, quiltmaker and quilting teacher, Dayton, Ohio
Lari Ehni, fiber artist, Houston, Texas
Jacqueline Enthoven, author, lecturer, craftswoman, and designer, Santa Barbara, California
Robbie Fanning, publisher, author of *Decorative Machine Stitchery*, Menlo Park, California
Gayle M. Feller, artist, teacher, and craftsperson, San Jose, California
Ilene Ferrini-Tuttle, painter and exhibiting tapestry designer, Carmel, California
Shirley Fink, weaver, teacher, wife, mother, friend, and person, Auburndale, Massachusetts
Norene Firth, writer, teacher, and artist, San Diego, California
Patricia B. Foley, fiber designer, Portland, Oregon
Paula Foster, artist, Davis, California
Elizabeth Fuller, batik artist, designer, and teacher, Claremont, California
Catherine Gibson, artist, San Rafael, California
Joyce Gross, writer and teacher, Mill Valley Quilt Authority, Mill Valley, California
Beth Gutcheon, co-author of *The Perfect Patchwork Primer* and *The Quilt Design Workbook*, New York, New York
Carolyn Vosburg Hall, teacher, artist, and author of *Stitched and Stuffed Art*, Birmingham, Michigan
Kitt Heidel, administrator-teacher, Bloomfield Hills, Michigan
Cindy Hickok, fiber artist, Houston, Texas
Gini Hill, fiber artist and teacher, Houston, Texas
Ginny Hoag, stitchery artist and teacher, La Cañada, California
Doris Hoover, stitcher, quilter, and teacher, Palo Alto, California
Nancy Hoskins, fiber artist, Eugene, Oregon
Jody House, fiber designer, author of *Needlepoint Boxes*, Davis, California
Constance Howard, artist and author of *Inspiration for Embroidery* and *Embroidery and Colour*, London, England
Mary Ellen Hritz, weaver/craftsman, Youngstown, Ohio
Karen Jahncke, designer and doll maker, New Orleans, Louisiana
Marilyn Judson, calligrapher, stitcher, and author, Davis, California

Barbara C. Kelley, batik artist, Detroit, Michigan
Barbara Kensler, soft-sculpture artist and teacher, Eugene, Oregon
Bucky King, threadbender and fiber artist, Sheridan, Wyoming
Pat King, stitchery artist, Houston, Texas
Tricia Klem, batik and fiber arts, San Luis Obispo, California
Kaethe Kliot, lace artist, teacher, and author of *Bobbin Lace,* Berkeley, California
Lynda Lanker, painter and textile artist, Eugene, Oregon
Ann La Pietra, toymaker and owner of The Kids' Place, Glen Ellyn, Illinois
Ruth Law, toy- and doll maker and co-author of *Handmade Toys and Games*, Claremont, California
Joan Lewis, stitcher and teacher, The Dalles, Oregon
Nancy Lipe, fiber artist, Stanford, California
Sharon Lappin Lumsden, weaver, wife, mother, teacher, all-around good person, Champaign, Illinois
Jorjanna Lundgren, designer/craftsman, La Jolla, California
Elsa E. Mann, stitchery teacher, Beaverton, Oregon
K. Lee Manuel, exhibiting artist and teacher, Santa Cruz, California
Carol Martin, artist and designer, San Diego, California
Gloria McNutt, stitcher and doll maker, Visalia, California
Dona Meilach, artist, teacher, author of numerous craft books, including *Boxed Art* and *How to Create Your Own Designs*, San Diego, California
Joan Michaels-Paque, fiber artist, teacher, author, Shorewood, Wisconsin
Bea Miller, stitchery artist and teacher, Los Altos, California
Reta Miller, artist and craftsperson, Salem, Oregon
Jo Morris, quilter, owner of Quiltworks, Granville, New York
Dee Mosteller, quilter, writer for TV and magazines, co-author of *Trapunto and Other Raised Quilting*, New York, New York
Peggy Moulton, stitcher, Orinda, California
Barbara Murdock, artist, art teacher, and quilt designer, Sparks, Nevada
Momo Nagano, weaver, Los Angeles, California
Barbara Neill, fabric artist and craftsman, Eugene, Oregon
Maryellen Nix, exhibiting artist and printmaker
Jill Nordfors, exhibiting artist and author of *Needle Lace and Needle Weaving*, Gig Harbor, Washington
Birgetta Bernt Olsen, designer, Davis, California
Nancy Papa, textile artist and writer, Los Gatos, California
Jerrie Peters, crafts designer and fiber artist, Fresno, California
Florence Pettit, artist, author of *How to Make Whirligigs and Whimmey Diddles*, Glenbrook, Connecticut
Ellen Phillips, clay and fiber artist, La Mesa, California
Yvonne Porcella, mother, nurse, weaver, designer, and teacher, Modesto, California
Elsbeth Ramos, fiber artist, Monterey, California
Jo Reimer, fiber artist and teacher, Portland, Oregon
Helen W. Richards, artist and teacher, Laguna Beach, California
Joyce Richards, fiber artist, Bloomingdale, Illinois
Peggy Ritsi, teacher and shopowner, Dana Point, California
Judy Roderick, batik artist, Albuquerque, New Mexico
Carol Cheney Rome, designer, teacher, author of *A New Look at Needlepoint*, and co-author of *Needlepoint Letters and Numbers*
Bev Rush, stitcher, photographer, and author of *The Stitchery Idea Book*, Federal Way, Washington
Cathy Ryan, fiber designer and co-author of *The Banner Book: How to Sew a Celebration*
Joan Schulze, exhibiting artist and teacher, Sunnyvale, California
Beatrice Sheftel, teacher and artist, Manchester, Connecticut
Barbara Smith, fiber artist and teacher, Glen Ellyn, Illinois
Wilcke H. Smith, fiber artist and teacher, Albuquerque, New Mexico
Lee Erlin Snow, artist, teacher and co-author of *Creative Stitchery* and *Weaving Off-Loom*, Los Angeles, California
Cam Smith Solari, photographer and teacher, Los Angeles, California
Elyse Sommer, craftsperson, lecturer, writers' agent, and author of numerous books, including *Wearable Crafts* and *Career Opportunities in Crafts*, Woodmere, New York
Mary Spraque, artist and teacher, St. Louis, Missouri

June Steinbaugh, weaver and partner in Weavers Workshop, New Orleans, Louisiana
DeLoris Stude, quilter and teacher, owner of Grandmother's Flower Garden Quilt Shop, Portland, Oregon
Rivkah Sweedler, weaver and fiber artist, Gig Harbor, Washington
Anne Syer, batik artist, San Luis Obispo, California
Barbara Threefoot, weaver, Weavers Workshop, River Ridge, Louisiana
Maggie Turner, stitcher, Portland, Oregon
Eleanor A. Van de Water, artist and teacher, Vancouver, Washington
Jackie Vermeer, author of *The Little Kids Craft Book* and *American Crafts*, Sand Point, Idaho
Kathy Vidak, homemaker, teacher, and craftsman, Visalia, California
Sally Wetherby, craftswoman, California
Nancy Wettlaufer, potter, co-author of *The Craftsman's Survival Manual*, Skaneateles, New York
Barbara Wheeler, craftsman, Augusta, Georgia
Erica Wilson, teacher, designer, and author of numerous books on needlecraft, including *Needleplay* and *Crewel Embroidery*, New York, New York
Jean Wilson, weaver, teacher, and author of numerous weaving books, including *Weaving You Can Wear* and *Weaving You Can Use*, Bellevue, Washington
Yvette Woods, exhibiting artist and teacher, St. Louis, Missouri

and many others.

And to these women who have so willingly offered help and guidance from their professional points of view, I am most grateful and appreciative:

Marjorie Anneberg, The Anneberg Gallery, San Francisco, California
Barbara Brabec, publisher of *Artisan Crafts* and *Craftspirit*, Illinois
Evelyn J. Brannon, Butterick Publishing Company
Theresa Capuana, *Woman's Day* Magazine
Fredrica Daugherty, *Decorating and Crafts*
Gertrude Dieken, *Farm Journal* Magazine
Margo Garrity, *Better Homes and Gardens*
Alyson Smith Gonsalves, Sunset Books
Nancy Newman Green, Van Nostrand Reinhold Publishing Company
Deborah Harding, *Family Circle* Magazine
Marilyn Heise, editor and publisher, *The Working Craftsman*
Mollie Kerr, *Fibernews*
Harriet Lyons, editor
Rachel Martens, editor
Nance O'Banion, FiberWorks Center for the Textile Arts, Berkeley, California
Marian Sanders, Rusty Needle (Gallery), Laguna Beach, California
Julie Schafler, Julie: Artisans' Gallery, Inc., New York, New York
Karen Van Westering, Doubleday and Company
Terry Taplinger, Taplinger Publishing Company
Sandra Wooten, Dabadaba (Gallery), Albany, California

and many others.

Index

age of crafts person in relation to career, 79,
108
agents for writers of crafts material, 132–133
American Crafts Council, 116, 117
American Crayon Company, 107
attitudes toward creative work, craftswoman's, 25
See also men *and* roles

babysitters, 47, 54
babysitting pools or co-ops, 47–49, 54
Better Homes and Gardens annuals, 124
books on crafts, writing and publishing,
97–98, 130–133
business information publications for crafts
people, 115, 116, 123

Career Opportunities in Crafts (Sommer),
117
centering, concept of, 83–84 ff., 89
Centering (M. C. Richards), 83
children and child care, creative careers
in relation to, 5, 6–7, 10, 11, 13, 14, 16,
34, 38–39, 73–74, 76–78
commissions, obtaining and executing, 120–
122
consignment sales of craft work, 118–119
Contemporary Craft Market Place (American
Crafts Council), 117
Contemporary Crafts Museum (New York
City), 107
contact between crafts workers, importance
of 78–79
cooperative galleries for showing craft work,
119–120
copying of original work, unethical, 126–
127
copyrighting to protect original creative
work, 127
Countryside Living and *Farm Journal*
magazine, 125
Crafts Horizons magazine, 127
*Craftsmen in Business: A Guide to Financial
Management and Taxes* (Connaughton),
116

Daugherty, Frederica, 125
decision-making about crafts careers, 20, 43,
63, 84–85
and children, 50, 63
Decorating and Craft Ideas magazine, 125

designs, selling, 122–123
to magazines, 123–127
Dieken, Gertrude, 125
direct sales of craft work, 120
donating creative works for charity, 111

Eastern States Quilt Exposition, 107
emergencies in meeting deadlines, coping
with, 14, 98
exhibiting work, seeking opportunities and
places for, 107, 117–122
exposure, public, of creative work, 106–109

fairs and craft shows, selling creative work
at, 120
Family Circle magazine, 124, 127
family cooperation in household management, necessity of, 16–17, 34, 36–37,
39, 54–55, 76, 77
and child care, 46, 78
Feminine Mystique, The (Friedan), 17
fiber arts, careers in, 4–5, 6–7, 8
See also decision-making *and* homemaking
and roles
Fibernews magazine, 125

gallery exhibitions, 117
Garrity, Margo, 124
Gift From the Sea (Lindbergh), 87
giving away creative work, 116
Gonsalves, Alyson Smith, 126, 132

Harding, Deborah, 124, 125, 126
Heise, Marilyn, 125
homemaking and creative careers, conflicts
in combining, 6–7, 10–11, 12–13, 14,
16–20, 24, 33–40, 98
House Beautiful magazine, 107
household help, hired, value of, 34, 36, 37,
48–49, 56, 78
See also babysitters
husbands or partners, *see* men

ideas, creative, sources of, 88–93
identity, professional, developing, 85–87
identity of the woman as creative person,
see decision-making *and* roles
illustrating books on crafts, 133
income from creative work, attitudes toward, 105–106, 135–136
interruptions, coping with, 51, 53

joint ventures in crafts production, 134–135

Kerr, Mollie, 125
kits, designing and marketing, 122, 123

Ladies Home Journal magazine, 12
lecturing as profitable adjunct to creative
   work, 41–42, 80, 129–130
Lindbergh, Anne Morrow, 87

magazine articles of crafts, writing, 133–134
marketing products of creative work, 110–
   122 *passim*
men, career woman's relationships with, 5,
   7, 11, 12, 14, 16, 46, Chapter 5, 75
Mill Valley Quilt Authority, 40

noise, coping with, 51, 54

pets, problems of, 76–77
presentation of creative work to promote
   sales, 110
pressure, working under, 95–96 ff.
pricing creative work, 110–112
   according to function, 112
   according to subject evaluation, 115
   according to time spent, 113–115
   by the square foot, 112–113
professionalism in creative careers, 109–
   110 ff.

questionnaire for craftswomen, 137–139

Ramos, Ann, 123
"real work," general misconception of, 43,
   67, 75
record keeping for home craft businesses,
   116–117, 120
resumés, writing professional, 109–110
roles, changes in and definitions of women's,
   4–6, 8, 11, 13, 65, 85
   See also identity, professional

self-esteem in relation to creative careers,
   110
   See also decision-making *and* roles
self-imposition of housekeeping standards,
   needless, 37–40
   See also homemaking

self-support in creative careers, unlikelihood
   of, 6
   See also income
selling creative products, 106, 110–122
Selling Your Crafts (Nelson), 117
shops and other buyers of creative work,
   dealing with, 113–114, 119
single living status of career women, 5, 46,
   62–63
Small Business Administration, 115
storage space for work materials and projects, 26, 27–30
studio at home, advantages and disadvantages
   of, 6–7, 10, 11, 23–27, 50, Chapter 5,
   75, 114
   See also children *and* homemaking
studio away from home, advantages of, 24–
   25
Sunset Books, 126

Taplinger, Terry, 132
Taplinger Publishing Company, 132
Tax Guide for Small Business (U.S. Treasury
   Dept., Internal Revenue Service), 116
Taxes and the Artist (Artists Equity), 116
teaching as adjunct to creative career, 41–42,
   72, 73, 74, 105, 127–129
time, priorities in use of, 38–43
   See also Chapter 1 *and* children
Time magazine, 123
trading creative work for needs and services,
   116

U.S. Department of Labor, 115

Visual Artist and the Law, The, 116

Woolf, Virginia, 25
Working Craftsman, The magazine, 20, 59,
   125
working time, 11–13
   breaking down, to ease deadline pressure,
      100
   estimating, for commissions, 121
   in relation to deadlines, 98
   organizing and using, 14–20
Wright, Roxa, 107
writing crafts articles for magazines, 133–134
writing crafts books, 97–98, 130–133